Dawn Staley: Rising above

"DAWN STALEY: RISING ABOVE"

DAWN STALEY: RISING ABOVE

All rights reserved. No part of this publication may be reproduced, distributed, or transmitted in any form or by any means, including photocopying, recording, or other electronic or mechanical methods, without the prior written permission of the publisher, except in the case of brief quotations embodied in critical reviews and certain other noncommercial uses permitted by copyright law.

Copyright © 2024 by Pamela A. Rameriz

"DAWN STALEY: RISING ABOVE"

A Journey From North Philly Streets to Global Basketball Icon, Transforming Women's Basketball and Inspiring Generations

PAMELA A RAMERIZ

Table of Contents

Introduction

chapter 1. Early Life in Philadelphia
Family Background and Childhood Influences

Chapter 2. Discovering Basketball
Introduction to the Game and Early Passion

Chapter 3. High School Years
Rising Star at Dobbins Technical High School

Chapter 4. College Journey at Virginia
Recruiting, Challenges, and Triumphs at UVA

Chapter 5. Olympic Glory
Representing Team USA and Winning Gold Medals

Chapter 6. WNBA Career
Professional Playing Career and Impact

Chapter 7. Transition to Coaching
Early Coaching Experiences and Challenges

Chapter 8. Building a Coaching Legacy
Leadership at Temple University and Beyond

Chapter 9. National Team Coaching
Guiding Team USA to Success on the International Stage

Chapter 10. Off the Court
Philanthropy, Community Involvement, and Personal Life

Chpater 11. Impact on Women's Basketball

Contributions to the Sport and Athlete Empowerment

Chapter 12. Achievements and Awards
Career Highlights, Honors, and Records

Conclusion

Appendix: Timeline of Dawn Staley's Career

INTRODUCTION

Dawn Staley stands as one of the most influential figures in the world of basketball, renowned not only for her prowess on the court but also for her transformative impact as a coach and advocate. Her journey from the bustling streets of North Philadelphia to the upper echelons of basketball success is a narrative filled with determination, resilience, and an unyielding passion for the game.

Born on May 4, 1970, in Philadelphia, Pennsylvania, Dawn Michelle Staley emerged from humble beginnings. Raised in a working-class household by her mother, Estelle, alongside her four siblings, Staley's early years were marked by financial struggles and a strong sense of community.

Estelle, a single mother, worked tirelessly to provide for her family, instilling in Dawn the values of hard work, perseverance, and the importance of education. These foundational principles would become cornerstones of Staley's life and career.

Philadelphia, known for its rich history and diverse culture, provided a unique backdrop for Dawn's formative years. The city's vibrant yet challenging environment shaped her character and ambitions.

North Philadelphia, in particular, with its economic hardships and vibrant community spirit, played a crucial role in Dawn's early development. The local playgrounds and community centers served as her training grounds, where she spent countless hours honing her skills and cultivating a deep love for basketball.

From an early age, it was evident that Dawn possessed an extraordinary talent for basketball. Her innate ability to handle the ball, combined with her quickness and court vision, set her apart from her peers.

The competitive nature of the street basketball scene in Philadelphia demanded toughness and resilience, qualities that would become hallmarks of Staley's playing style. Her early experiences on the neighborhood courts instilled in her a fearless approach to the game and an unwavering determination to succeed.

As Dawn's talent blossomed, she began to attract attention from local coaches and mentors who recognized her potential. One such mentor was John Chaney, the legendary coach of Temple University's men's basketball team. Chaney's tough-love approach and emphasis on discipline and defense resonated with Dawn. Under his guidance, she learned the importance of mental toughness, teamwork, and strategic thinking—principles that would later define her coaching philosophy.

Dawn's journey through high school further solidified her status as a rising star. Attending Murrell Dobbins Technical High School, she led her team to multiple city championships, showcasing her leadership and playmaking abilities.

Her performances on the court were electrifying, earning her accolades and attracting the attention of college recruiters from across the nation. Dawn's success at Dobbins was a source of pride for her community, inspiring other young athletes to pursue their dreams despite the challenges they faced.

Upon graduating from high school, Dawn's next chapter took her to the University of Virginia, where she played under the tutelage of coach Debbie Ryan. At UVA,

Staley's star continued to rise. She became a three-time Kodak All-American and received the Naismith College Player of the Year award.

Her impact on the college basketball scene was profound, leading the Cavaliers to three consecutive Final Four appearances and solidifying her reputation as one of the greatest players in NCAA history.

Staley's achievements extended beyond the collegiate level. She represented the United States in international competitions, including the 1996, 2000, and 2004 Olympic Games, where she won three gold medals.

Her contributions to Team USA were instrumental in cementing her legacy as a global ambassador for the sport of basketball. The Olympic stage provided Dawn with a platform to showcase her talents on a global scale and further expand her influence.

Transitioning from player to coach, Dawn embraced new challenges with the same tenacity that defined her playing career. She began her coaching journey at Temple University, where she inherited a program in need of revival.

Through her leadership and strategic acumen, Staley transformed the Owls into contenders, guiding them to multiple NCAA tournament appearances and earning recognition as a rising star in the coaching ranks. Her success at Temple paved the way for her next coaching endeavor at the University of South Carolina.

At South Carolina, Dawn Staley's coaching career reached new heights. Under her guidance, the Gamecocks achieved unprecedented success, including multiple

SEC championships and an NCAA national championship.

Staley's coaching philosophy, rooted in discipline, defense, and teamwork, resonated with her players and led to a culture of excellence. Her ability to mentor and develop young talent further cemented her reputation as one of the most respected coaches in the game.

Staley's impact extends far beyond the basketball court. She has been a staunch advocate for gender equality in sports, championing the cause of increased opportunities and resources for female athletes.

Her commitment to empowering the next generation of basketball players, particularly young women of color, underscores her role as a trailblazer and role model in the sports community. Dawn's advocacy efforts have helped to break down barriers and pave the way for future generations of female athletes.

In recognition of her contributions to the sport, Dawn Staley has received numerous honors and awards throughout her career. From being inducted into the Naismith Memorial Basketball Hall of Fame to receiving the prestigious USA Basketball National Coach of the Year award, her accolades reflect her profound impact on the game. Yet, despite her many achievements, Dawn remains grounded and focused on her mission to inspire and uplift others.

Dawn Staley's journey is not just a story of personal triumph but also a narrative of resilience, community, and the transformative power of sport. Her rise from the streets of North Philadelphia to the pinnacle of basketball success serves as a testament to what can be achieved through hard work, dedication, and an unwavering belief in oneself. Dawn's story is one of breaking barriers, shattering stereotypes, and leaving an indelible mark on the world of sports.

As we embark on this exploration of Dawn Staley's life, we will delve into the pivotal moments and defining experiences that have shaped her remarkable career. From her early years in Philadelphia to her triumphs on the global stage, we will uncover the untold chapters of her extraordinary journey.

Join me as we celebrate the life and legacy of a true basketball legend, Dawn Staley, and discover the enduring lessons and inspirations that her story offers to us all.

CHAPTER 1

EARLY LIFE IN PHILADELPHIA

Family Background and Childhood Influences

Dawn Michelle Staley was born on May 4, 1970, in the bustling and vibrant city of Philadelphia, Pennsylvania. The city of Philadelphia, with its rich history and diverse culture, provided a unique backdrop for Dawn's formative years. It was here, in the North Philadelphia neighborhood, that Staley's journey to becoming one of basketball's most influential figures began.

Staley's upbringing was characterized by both love and struggle. She was the second youngest of five children in a single-parent household, raised by her mother, Estelle Staley. Estelle worked tirelessly as a customer service representative to provide for her family, often working long hours to make ends meet.

Despite the financial challenges they faced, Estelle's unwavering dedication to her children instilled in Dawn a profound sense of resilience and determination.

The Staley household was a close-knit unit, bound by the shared experience of overcoming adversity. Dawn's siblings—Lawrence, Anthony, Tracey, and Eric—played significant roles in her upbringing. The competitive and supportive environment created by her siblings fueled her passion for sports from an early age. The makeshift basketball games in their backyard and the intense pickup games on the neighborhood courts were where Dawn's love for basketball first took root.

Philadelphia, particularly North Philly, was not just a place but a crucible that shaped Staley's character and ambitions. The neighborhood, while economically challenged, was rich in community spirit and resilience. The local playgrounds and community centers served as gathering places where young people could engage in sports and find camaraderie.

For Dawn, these courts became her sanctuary. The rough-and-tumble nature of street basketball in Philadelphia required a toughness and tenacity that would later become hallmarks of her playing style.

From an early age, Staley demonstrated an extraordinary talent for basketball. Her innate ability to handle the ball, her quickness, and her court vision set her apart from her peers. But it wasn't just her physical skills that stood out; it was her competitive spirit and relentless drive. Whether playing against boys or older children, Dawn's determination to prove herself fueled her to push beyond her limits. Her early experiences on the Philadelphia courts laid the foundation for the fearless and relentless competitor she would become.

Dawn's mother, Estelle, played a pivotal role in nurturing her budding talent. Recognizing her daughter's passion and potential, Estelle made sure that Dawn had access to opportunities to play and develop her skills. Despite the family's limited financial resources, Estelle's support was unwavering.

She encouraged Dawn to pursue her dreams, emphasizing the importance of hard work and perseverance. Estelle's belief in Dawn's abilities provided a crucial source of motivation and confidence.

As Dawn continued to hone her skills, she began to attract attention from local coaches and mentors who recognized her potential. One of the most significant influences in her early basketball development was John Chaney, the legendary coach of Temple University's men's basketball team.

Chaney, known for his tough-love approach and emphasis on discipline, saw something special in the young Staley. He took her under his wing, offering guidance and mentorship that would prove invaluable in her journey.

Under Chaney's tutelage, Dawn's understanding of the game deepened. He taught her the importance of defense, teamwork, and mental toughness—principles that would become cornerstones of her playing and coaching philosophy. Chaney's influence extended beyond the technical aspects of the game; he instilled in Dawn a sense of purpose and a belief that basketball could be a vehicle for personal and social change.

Dawn's burgeoning talent and determination soon began to pay off. By the time she reached high school, she was already a standout player, known throughout Philadelphia for her exceptional skills and competitive spirit. She enrolled at Murrell Dobbins Technical High School, where she would further cement her reputation as a rising star in the world of basketball.

At Dobbins, Staley's impact was immediate and profound. She led her high school team to multiple city championships, showcasing her leadership and playmaking abilities. Her performances on the court were electrifying, earning her accolades and catching the attention of college recruiters from across the country.

Dawn's success at Dobbins was not just a personal achievement but a source of pride for her community, inspiring other young athletes to pursue their dreams despite the challenges they faced.

Beyond the basketball court, Dawn's experiences in North Philadelphia shaped her worldview and sense of identity. The neighborhood's challenges—poverty, crime, and limited opportunities—were stark realities that she and her peers navigated daily.

These experiences instilled in Dawn a deep sense of empathy and a commitment to giving back to her community. She understood that her success could serve as a beacon of hope and a testament to what could be achieved through hard work and determination.

Dawn's early years were also influenced by the broader social and cultural dynamics of the time. Growing up in the 1970s and 1980s, she witnessed significant changes in the landscape of women's sports. The passage of Title IX in 1972, which prohibited sex-based discrimination in federally funded education programs and activities, opened up new opportunities for female athletes. However, the fight for equality in sports was far from over, and Dawn was acutely aware of the barriers that still existed for women, especially women of color.

Staley drew inspiration from pioneering female athletes who had paved the way before her. Legends like Cheryl Miller, Lynette Woodard, and Ann Meyers were trailblazers who shattered stereotypes and redefined what was possible for women in basketball.

Their achievements and struggles resonated deeply with Dawn, fueling her determination to make her own mark on the sport and contribute to the ongoing fight for gender equality.

As Dawn prepared to take the next steps in her basketball journey, the support of her family, community, and mentors provided a solid foundation. Her early years in Philadelphia were a crucible in which her talents were forged, her character was tested, and her dreams took shape. The lessons learned and the values instilled during this time would guide her through the challenges and triumphs that lay ahead.

In reflecting on her early years, Dawn often speaks of the profound influence of her mother, Estelle. Estelle's unwavering support and sacrifices were instrumental in Dawn's development as both an athlete and a person.

She instilled in Dawn a belief that anything was possible with hard work, dedication, and a relentless pursuit of excellence. This belief would become a driving force in Dawn's life, propelling her to achieve greatness on and off the court.

Dawn's journey from the streets of North Philadelphia to the heights of basketball success is a testament to the power of community, family, and determination. Her early years were marked by challenges and opportunities, influences, and inspirations that shaped her into the person and leader she would become.

As we continue to explore Dawn Staley's remarkable life, it is clear that her roots in Philadelphia provided the foundation for a legacy that continues to inspire and uplift generations of athletes and fans alike.

CHAPTER 2

DISCOVERING BASKETBALL

Introduction to the Game and Early Passion

Dawn Staley's love affair with basketball began in the vibrant and challenging environment of North Philadelphia, a place where community spirit thrived despite economic hardships. This neighborhood, with its concrete courts and fervent basketball culture, served as the crucible where Dawn's remarkable journey in the sport commenced. Her introduction to the game and the early passion that ignited her basketball career were influenced by a confluence of personal determination, family support, and community involvement.

Early Influences and Introduction to Basketball

Dawn Michelle Staley was born on May 4, 1970, into a close-knit family headed by her mother, Estelle Staley. Estelle, a single mother of five, worked tirelessly to provide for her children, emphasizing the importance of education and hard work. Growing up in such an environment instilled in Dawn a sense of resilience and determination that would become hallmarks of her character.

The bustling streets of North Philadelphia were home to numerous playgrounds and community centers, which played a pivotal role in Dawn's introduction to basketball. These urban courts were more than just recreational spaces; they were the heart of the community, where children gathered to play, compete, and forge lifelong friendships. For Dawn, these courts became a sanctuary and a proving ground.

Dawn's first encounters with basketball were informal and unstructured. She often joined her older brothers, Lawrence and Anthony, in their pickup games. Playing against boys who were older and stronger honed her competitive edge and physical toughness. These early experiences were crucial in developing her skills and instilling in her a relentless drive to excel.

The Role of Family in Fostering Passion

Dawn's family played a significant role in nurturing her budding passion for basketball. Despite financial constraints, Estelle ensured that her children had access to recreational activities that would keep them engaged and out of trouble. She recognized Dawn's enthusiasm for basketball and supported her participation in local leagues and community programs.

Dawn's siblings also contributed to her development as a basketball player. The sibling rivalries and backyard games were intense and competitive, pushing Dawn to improve her skills and stamina. These interactions taught her valuable lessons about perseverance, teamwork, and resilience. The familial support and encouragement provided a strong foundation for Dawn's burgeoning basketball career.

Community Support and Early Opportunities

The community of North Philadelphia was

instrumental in Dawn's early basketball journey. Local coaches, mentors, and older players recognized her talent and provided guidance and opportunities for growth. One notable figure was John Chaney, the legendary coach of Temple University's men's basketball team. Chaney's tough-love approach and emphasis on discipline resonated with Dawn, shaping her understanding of the game and influencing her coaching philosophy in later years.

The community centers and recreational leagues offered structured environments where Dawn could refine her skills. These programs not only provided coaching and competition but also instilled values of sportsmanship, leadership, and commitment. Dawn's participation in these leagues allowed her to compete against talented peers, further fueling her passion for the game.

Developing Skills and Building Confidence

As Dawn immersed herself in basketball, her skills began to flourish. Her quickness, ball-handling ability, and court vision set her apart from her peers. She spent countless hours practicing, often rising early to work on her dribbling and shooting before school. Her dedication to improving her game was evident to everyone around her.

Dawn's competitive nature drove her to seek out challenges. She regularly played in neighborhood tournaments, where the competition was fierce and the stakes high. These experiences helped her develop a mental toughness and a fearless approach to the game. She learned to thrive under pressure and to use adversity as a catalyst for growth.

One of the key aspects of Dawn's early development was her ability to learn from every game and practice session. She was a keen observer, constantly studying the moves and techniques of other players. This analytical approach allowed her to incorporate new skills into her repertoire and to adapt her playing style to different situations.

High School Years: A Rising Star

Dawn's transition to high school marked a significant milestone in her basketball journey. She attended Murrell Dobbins Technical High School, where her talent quickly made her a standout player. Under the guidance of her high school coach, Dawn's game evolved to new heights. She led her team to multiple city championships, showcasing her leadership and playmaking abilities.

At Dobbins, Dawn's performances on the court were electrifying. She became known for her tenacity, skill, and ability to elevate her teammates' play. Her success at the high school level attracted attention from college recruiters nationwide, solidifying her reputation as one of the top prospects in the country.

The Influence of Role Models and Pioneers

As Dawn's passion for basketball grew, she drew inspiration from the achievements of pioneering female athletes who had blazed trails before her. Legends like Cheryl Miller, Lynette Woodard, and Ann Meyers were role models whose successes demonstrated the possibilities for women in basketball. Their stories of overcoming barriers and excelling in a male-dominated sport resonated deeply with Dawn.

These trailblazers not only inspired Dawn to pursue her dreams but also instilled in her a sense of responsibility to contribute to the advancement of women's sports. She recognized that her journey was part of a larger movement toward gender equality in athletics, and this awareness fueled her determination to succeed and to uplift others along the way.

Overcoming Challenges and Breaking Barriers

Dawn's journey was not without its challenges. Growing up in North Philadelphia, she faced the harsh realities of crime, poverty, and limited opportunities. These obstacles, however, only strengthened her resolve. Dawn learned to navigate these challenges with grace and resilience, using basketball as a means to rise above her circumstances.

In addition to external challenges, Dawn had to contend with societal expectations and gender stereotypes. As a young girl excelling in a sport traditionally dominated by males, she often faced skepticism and discrimination. Yet, she never allowed these barriers to deter her. Instead, she used them as motivation to prove her doubters wrong and to pave the way for future generations of female athletes.

The Crucible of Early Experiences

The experiences of Dawn's early years in Philadelphia were a crucible that forged her character and ambitions. The values instilled by her mother, the support of her family, the guidance of mentors, and the challenges she overcame all contributed to shaping her into the extraordinary athlete and leader she would become.

Dawn's early passion for basketball was not just about the love of the game; it was about finding a purpose and a sense of identity. The sport provided her with a platform to express herself, to challenge her limits, and to aspire to greatness. It was through basketball that Dawn discovered her potential and began to chart a path toward her dreams.

Conclusion: Laying the Foundation for Greatness

Dawn Staley's introduction to basketball and the early passion she developed for the game were the bedrock of her remarkable journey. The lessons learned and the values instilled during her formative years in North Philadelphia provided the foundation for a career that would transcend the sport itself.

As we continue to explore Dawn's life and achievements, it becomes clear that her early experiences were not just stepping stones but pivotal moments that defined her path to greatness.

Her story serves as an inspiration to young athletes everywhere, demonstrating that with hard work, resilience, and unwavering passion, it is possible to overcome any obstacle and achieve extraordinary success. Dawn Staley's legacy is a testament to the transformative power of sport and the enduring impact of a dream nurtured from humble beginnings.

CHAPTER 3

HIGH SCHOOL YEARS

Rising Star at Dobbins Technical High School

Dawn Staley's high school years at Murrell Dobbins Technical High School in Philadelphia mark a pivotal period in her journey to becoming a basketball legend. These years were filled with challenges, triumphs, and moments that defined her as an athlete and a leader.

This chapter delves into the experiences, influences, and milestones that shaped

Dawn's time at Dobbins and set the stage for her future success.

The Decision to Attend Dobbins Technical High School

Murrell Dobbins Technical High School, commonly known as Dobbins, was renowned for its strong academic and athletic programs. The decision for Dawn to attend Dobbins was influenced by a combination of its reputation, the opportunities it offered, and the guidance of her mentors and family. For Dawn, Dobbins represented a chance to further her education while also advancing her basketball career.

Dobbins Technical High School was located in North Philadelphia, not far from Dawn's home. The school was known for its commitment to providing students with vocational training and academic education, as well as a robust athletics program.

The school's basketball team had a history of success, and joining it would mean competing at a high level and gaining exposure to college recruiters and scouts.

Early Challenges and Adaptation

Transitioning from middle school to high school is a significant step for any teenager, and for Dawn, it came with its set of challenges. The academic demands of Dobbins, coupled with the rigorous training schedule of the basketball team, required Dawn to balance her studies and her sport effectively. She had to quickly adapt to the higher level of competition and the expectations placed on her both on and off the court.

One of the early challenges Dawn faced was adjusting to the physicality and pace of high school basketball. The games were faster, the opponents were stronger, and the stakes were higher. However, Dawn's innate talent, coupled with her relentless work ethic, allowed her to rise to the occasion. Her coaches and teammates quickly recognized her potential, and she began to make a name for herself as a formidable player.

Becoming a Team Leader

From the outset, Dawn's presence on the basketball team was transformative. Her skills, determination, and basketball IQ set her apart, and she quickly earned the respect of her coaches and teammates.

As a freshman, she made significant contributions to the team, displaying a level of maturity and poise uncommon for someone her age. Her leadership qualities began to shine through, and she was soon seen as a cornerstone of the team's future success.

By her sophomore year, Dawn had established herself as one of the team's leaders. Her ability to read the game, make crucial plays, and motivate her teammates earned her a leadership role both on and off the court. She led by example, demonstrating the importance of hard work, discipline, and teamwork. Her coaches relied on her to set the tone during practices and games, and her teammates looked up to her for guidance and inspiration.

Highlights of High School Career

Dawn Staley's high school basketball career was marked by numerous highlights and memorable moments that underscored her rising star status. Her performances in key games and tournaments drew attention from local and national media, as well as college scouts. Below are some of the standout achievements and milestones from her time at Dobbins Technical High School.

Leading Dobbins to Championships

One of the most significant accomplishments of Dawn's high school career was leading Dobbins to multiple city championships. Her leadership, scoring ability, and defensive prowess were instrumental in the team's success.

Each championship run was marked by thrilling games, clutch performances, and the unwavering support of the Dobbins community. Dawn's ability to perform under pressure and elevate her game during crucial moments became a defining characteristic of her high school career.

Personal Accolades and Recognition

Dawn's exceptional performances did not go unnoticed. She received numerous individual awards and honors, including All-City and All-State selections. Her scoring records, assist totals, and defensive statistics placed her among the elite high school players in the country. Dawn's accolades were a testament to her hard work, dedication, and the support of her coaches and teammates.

Memorable Games and Clutch Performances

Throughout her high school career, Dawn delivered numerous memorable performances that left a lasting impact on those who witnessed them. One such game was a city championship match where Dawn led Dobbins to a come-from-behind victory with a series of clutch shots and defensive stops. Her ability to remain calm under pressure and deliver when it mattered most earned her the reputation of being a clutch performer.

Influence of Coaches and Mentors

Dawn Staley's development as a player and leader was significantly influenced by the guidance and mentorship she received from her coaches at Dobbins. The coaching staff recognized Dawn's potential early on and played a crucial role in nurturing her talents and helping her navigate the challenges of high school basketball.

Coach Lawrence "Larry" Cannon

One of the most influential figures in Dawn's high school career was Coach Lawrence "Larry" Cannon. A former professional basketball player, Cannon brought a wealth of experience and knowledge to the Dobbins program.

His coaching philosophy emphasized fundamentals, discipline, and mental toughness—principles that resonated deeply with Dawn. Coach Cannon saw in Dawn a rare combination of talent and determination, and he dedicated himself to helping her reach her full potential.

Under Coach Cannon's guidance, Dawn developed a more nuanced understanding of the game. He pushed her to expand her skill set, improve her decision-making, and embrace the responsibilities of leadership. Coach Cannon's mentorship extended beyond the basketball court; he served as a role model and advisor, offering valuable life lessons and support.

The Role of Community Support

The support of the North Philadelphia

community played an instrumental role in Dawn's high school success. The local community, proud of her achievements and the positive representation she brought to the neighborhood, rallied behind her. This support manifested in packed gyms for her games, local media coverage, and a sense of pride that extended beyond Dobbins High School.

The community's support provided Dawn with a strong foundation and a sense of belonging. The encouragement and recognition she received from local fans, family members, and mentors reinforced her determination to succeed. This network of support was a source of motivation, helping her navigate the challenges of high school and the pressures of being a rising star.

Balancing Academics and Athletics

Throughout her high school years, Dawn faced the challenge of balancing her academic responsibilities with her demanding basketball schedule. Dobbins Technical High School emphasized the importance of education, and Dawn was committed to excelling in both her studies and her sport. This balancing act required discipline, time management, and a strong work ethic.

Dawn's ability to excel academically while pursuing her basketball dreams was a testament to her determination and resilience. She understood that success in the classroom was just as important as success on the court, and she made a concerted effort to maintain high academic standards. Her dedication to her education was evident in her grades and her commitment to learning.

Recruitment and College Prospects

As Dawn's high school career progressed, her talent and achievements attracted the attention of college recruiters from across the country. Major universities and college basketball programs recognized her potential and sought to recruit her. The process of selecting a college was a significant decision for Dawn and her family, one that would shape the next chapter of her basketball journey.

Dawn's recruitment process was marked by visits from college coaches, offers of scholarships, and the opportunity to play at some of the most prestigious basketball programs in the nation. The University of Virginia emerged as a top contender, with its strong academic reputation and competitive basketball program. Dawn's decision to attend UVA was influenced by the support and guidance she received from her family, coaches, and mentors.

The Legacy of Dobbins Technical High School

Dawn Staley's time at Dobbins Technical High School left an indelible mark on both her and the school. Her success on the basketball court brought recognition and pride to Dobbins, inspiring future generations of students and athletes. Dawn's legacy at Dobbins is one of excellence, leadership, and community impact.

Her achievements at Dobbins paved the way for other young athletes to pursue their dreams, demonstrating that with hard work and determination, anything is possible. The school's basketball program continued to thrive, buoyed by the example set by Dawn and her teammates. Dawn's story became a source of inspiration and a reminder of the transformative power of sports.

Transitioning to College

As Dawn's high school career came to a close, she faced the transition to college with a mixture of excitement and anticipation. The move from Philadelphia to Charlottesville, Virginia, where she would attend the University of Virginia, represented a new chapter in her life. It was an opportunity to further her education, develop her basketball skills, and compete at the highest level of college basketball.

The transition to college brought new challenges and opportunities. Dawn had to adjust to a new environment, meet the academic demands of college coursework, and compete against some of the best players in the country. Her experiences at Dobbins had prepared her well for this next step, equipping her with the skills, confidence, and resilience needed to succeed.

Conclusion

Looking back on her high school years at Dobbins Technical High School, Dawn Staley's journey is one of growth, achievement, and transformation. These years were a critical period in her development as an athlete and a leader, shaping the person she would become. The lessons learned, the relationships formed, and the challenges overcome during her time at Dobbins provided a strong foundation for her future success.

Dawn's high school years were marked by a relentless pursuit of excellence, a commitment to her community, and a passion for the game of basketball. Her story is a testament to the power of hard work, determination, and the support of a dedicated community. It serves as an inspiration to young athletes everywhere, demonstrating that with the right mindset they can achieve their goals and dream.

CHAPTER 4

COLLEGE JOURNEY AT VIRGINIA

Recruiting, Challenges, and Triumphs at UVA

Dawn Staley's college years at the University of Virginia (UVA) are a testament to her perseverance, talent, and leadership. This period of her life was marked by intense competition, significant challenges, and numerous triumphs, both on and off the basketball court. Her journey at UVA not only solidified her status as a basketball legend but also laid the groundwork for her future career as a coach and mentor. This chapter explores Dawn's recruitment to UVA, the obstacles she faced, and the milestones she achieved during her college years.

The Recruitment Process

The recruitment process for Dawn Staley was a whirlwind of attention and offers from some of the most prestigious basketball programs in the country. As one of the top high school players in the nation, Dawn was heavily scouted by college coaches who recognized her potential to transform their programs.

Her decision to attend the University of Virginia was influenced by several factors, including the school's academic reputation, the quality of its basketball program, and the relationships she formed with the coaching staff.

Attracting Attention

During her high school years at Dobbins Technical High School, Dawn's extraordinary talent on the basketball court drew the attention of college recruiters nationwide. Her impressive performances in city championships, coupled with her leadership abilities, made her a highly sought-after recruit. College coaches visited her games, attended practices, and reached out to her family and mentors in hopes of convincing her to join their programs.

The Decision-Making Process

Selecting the right college was a significant decision for Dawn and her family. She had to consider various factors, including the school's academic offerings, the strength of its basketball program, the coaching staff, and the campus environment. The University of Virginia emerged as a top contender for several reasons. The school's strong academic reputation aligned with Dawn's commitment to education, and its competitive basketball program offered her the opportunity to play at a high level.

Dawn was also impressed by the coaching staff at UVA, particularly Head Coach Debbie Ryan. Coach Ryan's vision for the program, her coaching philosophy, and her genuine interest in Dawn's development as a player and a person resonated with Dawn and her family. The supportive and welcoming atmosphere at UVA played a crucial role in Dawn's decision to commit to the Cavaliers.

The Signing

Dawn's decision to sign with the University of Virginia was met with excitement and anticipation. Her commitment to UVA was seen as a significant coup for the program, as it signaled the arrival of a game-changing player who could elevate the team to new heights. The signing was a momentous occasion for Dawn, her family, and the UVA community, marking the beginning of an exciting new chapter in her basketball journey.

Early Challenges at UVA

Transitioning from high school to college basketball presented Dawn with a set of new challenges. The increased level of competition, the demands of college coursework, and the need to adapt to a new environment required Dawn to push herself to new limits. Despite these challenges, Dawn's resilience and determination enabled her to navigate this transition successfully.

Adapting to College Basketball

The pace and physicality of college basketball were a step up from what Dawn had experienced in high school. The games were faster, the opponents were stronger, and the level of competition was higher. Dawn had to quickly adapt to the rigors of college basketball, which included more intense practices, a demanding game schedule, and the expectation to perform at a consistently high level.

Dawn's work ethic and commitment to improvement helped her rise to the occasion. She dedicated herself to refining her skills, studying game footage, and learning from her coaches and teammates. Her ability to adapt and grow as a player was evident in her performances on the court, where she showcased her scoring ability, defensive prowess, and leadership qualities.

Balancing Academics and Athletics
Balancing the demands of academics and

athletics is a challenge faced by many student-athletes, and Dawn was no exception. The rigorous academic standards at UVA, combined with the commitments required by the basketball program, necessitated effective time management and discipline. Dawn was determined to excel both in the classroom and on the court, recognizing the importance of a well-rounded college experience.

Dawn's dedication to her studies was evident in her academic performance. She made a concerted effort to keep up with her coursework, seek help when needed, and maintain high academic standards. Her ability to balance these responsibilities was a testament to her determination and resilience.

Triumphs on the Court

Dawn Staley's college career at the

University of Virginia was marked by numerous triumphs and memorable moments. Her impact on the basketball program was profound, leading the Cavaliers to unprecedented success and earning her a place among the greatest players in college basketball history.

Leading the Cavaliers to Success

From the moment she stepped onto the court for UVA, Dawn made an immediate impact. Her leadership, skill, and competitive spirit were instrumental in transforming the Cavaliers into a powerhouse team. During her tenure at UVA, Dawn led the team to multiple NCAA Tournament appearances, including three consecutive Final Four berths.

Memorable Games and Performances

Dawn's college career was filled with standout performances that left a lasting impression on fans, teammates, and opponents alike. One such memorable game was the 1991 NCAA Final Four matchup against the University of Tennessee. Despite facing a formidable opponent, Dawn's leadership and clutch play helped the Cavaliers secure a thrilling victory, advancing to the national championship game.

Another notable performance was her 28-point effort in a crucial game against the University of Connecticut, showcasing her scoring ability and tenacity. Dawn's ability to deliver in high-pressure situations earned her the reputation of being a clutch performer, capable of changing the outcome of a game with her play.

Individual Accolades and Recognition

Dawn's exceptional performances on the

court did not go unnoticed. Throughout her college career, she received numerous individual accolades and honors that recognized her contributions to the game and her outstanding abilities as a player.

All-American Honors

Dawn was a three-time consensus First Team All-American, a testament to her consistent excellence and dominance in college basketball. These honors reflected her status as one of the top players in the country and underscored her impact on the game.

National Player of the Year

In 1991 and 1992, Dawn was named the National Player of the Year, further solidifying her legacy as one of the greatest players in college basketball history. These prestigious awards recognized her outstanding performances, leadership, and contributions to her team's success.

Virginia Sports Hall of Fame

In recognition of her remarkable college career, Dawn was inducted into the Virginia Sports Hall of Fame. This honor celebrated her achievements and contributions to the University of Virginia and the broader sports community.

Overcoming Adversity

Dawn Staley's journey at UVA was not without its share of adversity. She faced numerous challenges, both on and off the court, that tested her resilience and determination. However, Dawn's ability to overcome these obstacles and emerge stronger was a defining aspect of her college career.

Injuries and Setbacks

Like many athletes, Dawn experienced injuries that threatened to derail her progress. During her sophomore year, she suffered a knee injury that required surgery and extensive rehabilitation. The injury was a significant setback, but Dawn's determination to return to the court motivated her to work tirelessly in her recovery.

Her resilience paid off, and she returned to action stronger than ever. Dawn's ability to overcome physical setbacks and continue performing at a high level was a testament to her work ethic and mental toughness.

Academic Challenges

Balancing academics and athletics presented ongoing challenges for Dawn. The demands of her coursework, coupled with the rigors of the basketball season, required careful time management and a strong support system. Despite these challenges, Dawn remained committed to her education, seeking help from tutors and academic advisors when needed.

Her dedication to her studies was evident in her academic achievements, and she successfully completed her degree in Rhetoric and Communication Studies. Dawn's ability to excel both academically and athletically showcased her determination and discipline.

Impact on the UVA Community

Dawn Staley's impact extended beyond the basketball court. She became a beloved figure within the UVA community, known for her leadership, character, and contributions to the university. Her influence was felt not only by her teammates and coaches but also by the broader student body and faculty.

Role Model and Leader

Dawn's leadership and commitment to excellence made her a role model for her peers and younger athletes. She led by example, demonstrating the importance of hard work, discipline, and perseverance. Her positive attitude and dedication to her team inspired those around her and created a culture of success within the basketball program.

Community Engagement

Dawn was also actively involved in the UVA community, participating in various outreach and community service initiatives. She recognized the importance of giving back and used her platform to make a positive impact on others. Her involvement in community activities further endeared her to the UVA community and highlighted her commitment to making a difference.

Legacy at the University of Virginia

Dawn Staley's legacy at the University of Virginia is one of excellence, leadership, and lasting impact. Her contributions to the basketball program, her academic achievements, and her influence within the UVA community have left an indelible mark on the university.

Elevating the Basketball Program

Dawn's time at UVA elevated the women's basketball program to new heights. Her leadership and exceptional play led the Cavaliers to unprecedented success, including multiple Final Four appearances and a national championship game. Her impact on the program continues to be felt, as she set a standard of excellence for future generations of players.

Inspiring Future Generations

Dawn's story serves as an inspiration to young athletes everywhere. Her journey from North Philadelphia to the University of Virginia, and her success in the face of adversity, demonstrate the power of hard work, determination, and resilience. Dawn's legacy inspires future generations to pursue their dreams and overcome obstacles in their path.

Contributions to Women's Basketball

Dawn Staley's impact extends beyond her time at UVA and even her own career. She has been a pivotal figure in the advancement of women's basketball, both as a player and a coach. Her success at UVA helped raise the profile of women's college basketball, demonstrating that the sport deserved the same recognition and respect as men's basketball.

Transitioning to Professional Basketball

As her college career at the University of Virginia came to a close, Dawn Staley faced the next big transition: moving from college basketball to the professional level. This transition was filled with excitement, new challenges, and the promise of further achievements.

WNBA Draft and Early Professional Career

Dawn's exceptional performance at UVA made her a top prospect for professional basketball. She entered the Women's National Basketball Association (WNBA) draft with high expectations and was selected ninth overall by the Charlotte Sting in the 1999 WNBA Draft. This marked the beginning of a new chapter in her basketball journey.

Dawn quickly made her mark in the WNBA, bringing the same determination, skill, and leadership that defined her college career. Her transition to professional basketball was seamless, and she continued to excel on the court. Dawn's professional career included several All-Star selections, and she quickly became one of the league's standout players.

Leadership and Coaching Career

Dawn's influence on the game of basketball did not end with her playing career. After retiring from professional play, she transitioned into coaching, where she continued to make significant contributions to the sport.

Early Coaching Success

Dawn began her coaching career at Temple University, where she revitalized the women's basketball program. Her leadership and coaching abilities quickly became evident, and she led the team to multiple NCAA Tournament appearances. Dawn's success at Temple earned her widespread recognition and set the stage for her next major coaching opportunity.

South Carolina and National Championships

In 2008, Dawn was named head coach of the University of South Carolina women's basketball team. Under her leadership, the program experienced unprecedented success, including multiple Southeastern Conference (SEC) championships and national titles. Dawn's ability to recruit top talent, develop players, and build a winning culture solidified her reputation as one of the best coaches in the country.

Olympic Coaching Career

Dawn's coaching success extended to the international stage as well. She served as an assistant coach for the U.S. Women's National Team, helping lead the team to gold medals in the Olympics. In 2021, she was named head coach of the U.S. Women's National Team, a testament to her coaching acumen and leadership abilities.

Giving Back and Mentorship

Throughout her career, Dawn has remained committed to giving back to the community and mentoring the next generation of athletes. She established the Dawn Staley Foundation, which focuses on providing educational and athletic opportunities for underserved youth. Through her foundation, Dawn has made a lasting impact on countless young lives, offering them the tools and support they need to succeed.

Advocacy for Women's Sports

Dawn has also been a vocal advocate for women's sports, using her platform to push for greater equality and recognition. She has worked tirelessly to promote women's basketball, challenge stereotypes, and ensure that female athletes receive the respect and opportunities they deserve.

Reflection on UVA and Personal Growth

Looking back on her college years at the University of Virginia, Dawn Staley reflects on the experiences that shaped her as a player, a leader, and a person. Her time at UVA was marked by significant personal growth, overcoming challenges, and achieving remarkable success.

Gratitude for Support

Dawn often expresses gratitude for the support she received from her coaches, teammates, and the UVA community. The relationships she built during her college years played a crucial role in her development and success. Coach Debbie Ryan, in particular, had a profound impact on Dawn's career, serving as a mentor and guiding her through the ups and downs of college basketball.

Lessons Learned

The lessons Dawn learned at UVA have stayed with her throughout her life. The importance of hard work, resilience, and leadership were instilled in her during those formative years. These principles have guided her in her professional career and in her efforts to give back to the community.

Legacy and Lasting Impact

Dawn Staley's legacy at the University of Virginia is enduring. She remains one of the most celebrated athletes in the school's history, and her contributions to the basketball program are still remembered and honored. Her journey from UVA to the heights of professional and coaching success serves as an inspiration to current and future student-athletes.

UVA Honors and Recognition

The University of Virginia has honored Dawn in various ways, recognizing her outstanding achievements and contributions. Her jersey number, 24, was retired by UVA, a rare honor that highlights her impact on the program. Additionally, she has been inducted into the Virginia Sports Hall of Fame and other prestigious organizations, cementing her place in the history of UVA athletics.

Inspiration for Future Generations

Dawn's story continues to inspire young athletes, particularly girls and women who aspire to achieve greatness in sports. Her journey demonstrates that with talent, hard work, and perseverance, it is possible to overcome obstacles and reach the highest levels of success. Dawn's legacy at UVA serves as a beacon of hope and a source of motivation for those who follow in her footsteps.

Conclusion

Dawn Staley's college journey at the University of Virginia was a defining period in her life, marked by remarkable achievements, significant challenges, and enduring triumphs. Her recruitment to UVA, the obstacles she overcame, and the milestones she reached are all integral parts of her story.

Dawn's impact on the UVA basketball program, her contributions to the university community, and her legacy as one of the greatest players in college basketball history are a testament to her extraordinary talent and determination.

As Dawn continues to make her mark in the world of basketball, both as a coach and a mentor, her journey at UVA remains a foundational chapter in her incredible story. The lessons learned, the relationships built, and the triumphs achieved during her college years have shaped her into the leader and trailblazer she is today. Dawn Staley's legacy at the University of Virginia will continue to inspire and influence future generations for years to come.

CHAPTER 5

OLYMPIC GLORY

Representing Team USA and Winning Gold Medals

Dawn Staley's career is marked by extraordinary achievements, but her contributions to the U.S. Women's National Basketball Team stand out as a pinnacle of her journey. Her involvement with Team USA spans multiple Olympics, highlighting her exceptional talent, leadership, and dedication to the sport.

Dawn's commitment to representing her country on the international stage not only brought her personal accolades but also cemented her legacy as one of the greatest figures in women's basketball history.

The Beginnings of an International Career

Dawn's introduction to international basketball came early in her career, as her talents quickly drew the attention of national team selectors. Her journey with Team USA began long before her first Olympic appearance, rooted in her participation in various international competitions and her growing reputation as a formidable player.

Early International Competitions

Dawn first donned the Team USA jersey in

the early 1990s, competing in events like the World University Games and the FIBA World Championships. These competitions were crucial in shaping her international career, providing her with the experience and exposure necessary to compete at the highest level. Her performances in these early tournaments showcased her skills and adaptability, earning her a spot on the Olympic roster.

The 1996 Atlanta Olympics: A Golden Debut

The 1996 Summer Olympics in Atlanta were a historic event for many reasons, and for Dawn Staley, they marked her debut on the Olympic stage. This Olympics was particularly significant as it was held on home soil, adding an extra layer of excitement and pressure for Team USA.

Building the Dream Team

The 1996 U.S. Women's Basketball Team is often referred to as the "Dream Team" of women's basketball, featuring an array of talented players, including Lisa Leslie, Sheryl Swoopes, and Rebecca Lobo. The team was meticulously assembled to dominate the competition and elevate the status of women's basketball globally. Dawn's inclusion in this elite group was a testament to her skill and her ability to perform under pressure.

Training and Preparation

The preparation for the Atlanta Olympics was intense. The team underwent rigorous training camps and participated in numerous exhibition games to build chemistry and ensure peak performance. Dawn's leadership and experience were invaluable during this period, as she helped unify the team and foster a winning mentality.

Dominating the Competition

Team USA entered the 1996 Olympics with high expectations and did not disappoint. They dominated the competition, winning all their games with significant margins. Dawn played a crucial role in the team's success, contributing both offensively and defensively. Her playmaking abilities, defensive tenacity, and leadership on the court were instrumental in guiding the team to victory.

The Gold Medal Game

The climax of the 1996 Olympics came with the gold medal game against Brazil. The match was highly anticipated, with both teams showcasing exceptional talent. However, Team USA, led by their star-studded lineup and strategic gameplay, emerged victorious, securing the gold medal with a decisive win. For Dawn, standing on the podium and receiving her first Olympic gold medal was a dream come true and a defining moment in her career.

The 2000 Sydney Olympics: Maintaining Excellence

Following the triumph in Atlanta, Dawn continued to be a key player for Team USA. The 2000 Sydney Olympics presented another opportunity for her to showcase her talents and help her team achieve Olympic glory once again.

Continuing the Legacy

The 2000 U.S. Women's Basketball Team aimed to continue the legacy established in Atlanta. The roster included a mix of veterans and new talents, all dedicated to maintaining the team's dominance on the international stage. Dawn's role as a seasoned player and leader was crucial in navigating the challenges of the tournament.

Overcoming Challenges

The road to the gold medal in Sydney was not without its challenges. The competition was fierce, with teams like Australia and Russia posing significant threats. However, Team USA's preparation, teamwork, and resilience helped them overcome these obstacles. Dawn's experience and calm demeanor under pressure were vital in close games, providing stability and confidence to her teammates.

Securing Another Gold Medal

In the gold medal game, Team USA faced Australia, a formidable opponent playing on their home turf. The game was intense, with both teams battling fiercely for the top spot. Dawn's leadership and clutch performances were instrumental in securing a hard-fought victory, and Team USA once again stood atop the podium, celebrating their success and cementing their legacy.

The 2004 Athens Olympics: The Captain's Final Bow

The 2004 Athens Olympics held special significance for Dawn Staley. It was not only another opportunity to win gold but also marked the culmination of her illustrious Olympic career. As the captain of Team USA, Dawn's leadership and experience were more important than ever.

Leading by Example

Dawn's role as captain was multifaceted. She was responsible for leading by example, both on and off the court. Her work ethic, dedication, and positive attitude were infectious, inspiring her teammates to strive for excellence. As a seasoned veteran, she provided valuable insights and guidance to younger players, helping them navigate the pressures of the Olympics.

The Journey to Gold

Team USA faced formidable opponents throughout the 2004 Olympics, but their preparation and unity helped them overcome every challenge. Dawn's performance in key games was outstanding, as she demonstrated her playmaking abilities, defensive prowess, and leadership. Her presence on the court was a calming and motivating factor for the team.

The Gold Medal Game

The gold medal game in Athens saw Team USA facing Australia once again. The match was highly competitive, with both teams displaying exceptional skill and determination. Dawn's leadership shone brightly in this game, as she orchestrated the offense, made crucial defensive plays, and provided steady guidance. The game ended with Team USA victorious, securing Dawn's third Olympic gold medal.

Legacy and Impact

Dawn Staley's Olympic career is a testament to her talent, leadership, and dedication to the sport of basketball. Her contributions to Team USA go beyond the medals and victories; they encompass her role as a leader, mentor, and trailblazer in women's basketball.

Elevating Women's Basketball

Dawn's success with Team USA helped elevate the status of women's basketball, both in the United States and globally. Her performances on the international stage showcased the skill and competitiveness of female athletes, inspiring a new generation of players and fans. The visibility and respect gained from these achievements contributed to the growth and development of women's basketball.

Role Model and Mentor

Throughout her career, Dawn has been a role model and mentor to many young athletes. Her Olympic experiences provided her with a platform to inspire others, demonstrating the importance of hard work, perseverance, and leadership. Dawn's willingness to share her knowledge and experiences has helped shape the careers of numerous players who followed in her footsteps.

Contributions to USA Basketball

Dawn's contributions to USA Basketball extend beyond her playing days. She has remained involved in the national team program, serving as a coach and advisor. Her insights and leadership have been invaluable in developing and guiding the next generation of players. Dawn's commitment to excellence and her dedication to the sport continue to influence and inspire.

Reflecting on Olympic Glory

Reflecting on her Olympic career, Dawn Staley often speaks of the pride and honor she felt representing her country. The experiences, challenges, and triumphs of competing on the world stage are etched in her memory, shaping her into the leader and icon she is today.

The Significance of the Gold Medals

For Dawn, the gold medals symbolize more than just victories; they represent the culmination of years of hard work, sacrifice, and determination. Each medal carries a story of challenges overcome, teamwork, and the relentless pursuit of excellence. The pride of standing on the podium, hearing the national anthem, and sharing the moment with her teammates is a cherished memory.

Lifelong Friendships and Bonds

One of the most rewarding aspects of Dawn's Olympic journey is the lifelong friendships and bonds formed with her teammates. The shared experiences of training, competing, and achieving greatness together created strong connections and mutual respect. These relationships have endured beyond their playing days, continuing to enrich Dawn's life.

Dawn Staley's Enduring Legacy

Dawn Staley's Olympic glory is a significant

chapter in her extraordinary career. Her contributions to Team USA and her impact on the sport of basketball are profound and enduring. As a player, coach, and mentor, Dawn's legacy continues to inspire and influence future generations.

Celebrating Achievements

Dawn's Olympic achievements are celebrated and remembered as some of the greatest moments in women's basketball history. Her leadership, skill, and determination set a standard of excellence that continues to inspire young athletes. The recognition and respect she earned through her Olympic successes have solidified her place among the legends of the sport.

Ongoing Contributions

Even after her playing days, Dawn's contributions to basketball remain significant. As a coach, she continues to shape and develop the talents of young players, guiding them to achieve their own dreams. Her involvement with USA Basketball and her advocacy for women's sports ensure that her impact on the game will continue for years to come.

Conclusion

Dawn Staley's Olympic glory is a testament to her exceptional talent, leadership, and dedication to the sport of basketball. Her journey with Team USA, from her debut in Atlanta to her final bow in Athens, is marked by extraordinary achievements and unforgettable moments.

Dawn's legacy as an Olympic champion and a trailblazer in women's basketball is enduring, inspiring future generations to pursue excellence and embrace the spirit of competition. Her contributions to the sport and her impact on the lives of countless athletes ensure that her story will continue to be celebrated and remembered for generations to come.

CHAPTER 6

WNBA CAREER

Professional Playing Career and Impact

Dawn Staley's transition from an illustrious college career to the professional arena of the Women's National Basketball Association (WNBA) was seamless and groundbreaking. Her professional playing career not only showcased her exceptional talent and leadership but also had a lasting impact on the WNBA and women's basketball as a whole.

This exploration of Dawn Staley's WNBA career delves into her journey from draft day to retirement, highlighting her achievements, influence, and the legacy she built.

The Birth of the WNBA and Dawn Staley's Entry

The WNBA was founded in 1996, providing a professional platform for female basketball players in the United States. This league was a significant milestone for women's sports, offering athletes the opportunity to play professionally at home rather than overseas. Dawn Staley, having already achieved remarkable success at the University of Virginia and in international competitions, was poised to make a significant impact in this new league.

The 1999 WNBA Draft
Dawn Staley entered the 1999 WNBA Draft

with high expectations. Her college achievements and international experience made her a highly sought-after player. On draft day, the Charlotte Sting selected her with the ninth overall pick. This moment marked the beginning of her professional career in the WNBA, and she quickly set out to make her mark on the league.

Early Years with the Charlotte Sting

Dawn's early years with the Charlotte Sting were characterized by her exceptional playmaking abilities, leadership, and determination to elevate her team. Her presence on the court was immediately felt, as she brought a high level of skill and basketball IQ to the Sting.

Rookie Season
In her rookie season, Dawn Staley quickly

adapted to the professional level, showcasing her versatility and leadership. She averaged impressive numbers in points, assists, and steals, proving herself as a vital asset to the team. Her ability to control the game from the point guard position made her a standout player in the league, earning her respect from teammates and opponents alike.

Establishing Leadership

Dawn's leadership qualities were evident from the beginning of her WNBA career. As a seasoned player with extensive experience in college and international play, she naturally took on a leadership role within the Sting. Her ability to inspire and guide her teammates was crucial in building team cohesion and competitiveness.

On-Court Performance and Playing Style

Dawn Staley's playing style was a blend of exceptional court vision, defensive tenacity, and scoring ability. Her ability to read the game and make precise passes set her apart as one of the best point guards in the league. She was also known for her relentless defense, often guarding the opponent's best player and disrupting their offensive flow.

Playmaking and Court Vision

Dawn's playmaking abilities were unparalleled. She had an innate ability to see plays develop before they happened, allowing her to make precise passes and create scoring opportunities for her teammates. Her court vision and basketball IQ made her a formidable point guard, capable of orchestrating the offense with precision.

Defensive Tenacity
Defense was another hallmark of Dawn's

game. She was known for her aggressive and tenacious defense, often guarding the opposing team's best player. Her quick hands, anticipation, and ability to read the opponent's movements made her a defensive force. Dawn's defensive prowess was instrumental in setting the tone for her team's overall defensive strategy.

Scoring Ability

While Dawn was primarily known for her playmaking and defense, she was also a capable scorer. She had a reliable mid-range jumper and the ability to drive to the basket. Her scoring versatility added another dimension to her game, making her a well-rounded and complete player.

Achievements and Milestones with the Sting

Dawn Staley's time with the Charlotte Sting

was marked by numerous achievements and milestones. Her individual accolades and contributions to the team were significant in elevating the profile of the Sting and the WNBA.

All-Star Selections

Throughout her career, Dawn earned multiple WNBA All-Star selections. These honors were a testament to her consistent performance and impact on the league. Being named an All-Star placed her among the elite players in the WNBA, highlighting her influence and excellence on the court.

Leading the Sting to Success

Dawn played a crucial role in leading the Charlotte Sting to several successful seasons. Her leadership and on-court performance were instrumental in guiding the team to the playoffs. One of the most memorable achievements was the Sting's run to the WNBA Finals in 2001. Although they fell short of winning the championship, Dawn's performance throughout the playoffs was exemplary, showcasing her ability to elevate her game in crucial moments.

Transition to the Houston Comets

In 2005, Dawn Staley was traded to the Houston Comets. This move marked a new chapter in her professional career. The Comets were a team with a rich history of success, and Dawn's addition brought experience and leadership to the squad.

Continuing Excellence

Dawn continued to excel with the Houston Comets, maintaining her high level of play and leadership. Her ability to adapt to a new team and contribute immediately was a testament to her professionalism and skill. She played a vital role in guiding the Comets to the playoffs and continued to earn respect as one of the league's premier point guards.

Mentorship and Influence

In Houston, Dawn took on an even more pronounced mentorship role. Her experience and leadership were invaluable to the younger players on the team. She provided guidance, shared her knowledge of the game, and helped develop the next generation of talent. Dawn's influence extended beyond her on-court performance, as she played a key role in shaping the team's culture and work ethic.

The Impact of Dawn Staley's WNBA Career

Dawn Staley's WNBA career had a profound impact on the league and the sport of women's basketball. Her contributions went beyond individual accolades and team success, as she played a crucial role in elevating the status and visibility of women's basketball.

Elevating the WNBA

Dawn's presence in the WNBA helped elevate the league's profile. Her exceptional talent, leadership, and sportsmanship made her a role model for young athletes and fans. Dawn's performances drew attention to the league and helped build a strong following for women's basketball. Her influence was instrumental in growing the WNBA and increasing its popularity.

Advocacy for Women's Sports

Throughout her career, Dawn was a vocal advocate for women's sports. She used her platform to push for greater recognition and equality for female athletes. Dawn's advocacy efforts were vital in challenging stereotypes and promoting the importance of supporting women's sports. Her work off the court complemented her on-court achievements, making her a significant figure in the advancement of women's basketball.

Legacy of Leadership

Dawn's legacy in the WNBA is deeply rooted in her leadership. Her ability to inspire and guide her teammates left a lasting impact on every team she played for. Dawn's leadership style was characterized by her work ethic, dedication, and positive attitude. She led by example, setting a standard of excellence that others aspired to follow. Her legacy as a leader continues to influence players and coaches in the league.

Retirement and Transition to Coaching

Dawn Staley's retirement from professional play marked the end of an era but also the beginning of a new chapter in her basketball journey. Her transition to coaching allowed her to continue making significant contributions to the sport.

Announcing Retirement

Dawn announced her retirement from the WNBA in 2006, after an illustrious career that spanned several years and included numerous accolades. Her retirement was a moment of reflection and celebration, as the league honored her contributions and legacy. While stepping away from playing professionally, Dawn's passion for the game remained undiminished.

Coaching Career Beginnings

Even before her retirement from the WNBA, Dawn had already begun her coaching career. In 2000, she became the head coach of the Temple University women's basketball team. Her transition to coaching was seamless, as she brought the same intensity, knowledge, and leadership to her coaching role. Dawn's success at Temple laid the foundation for her future coaching endeavors.

Legacy and Lasting Impact

Dawn Staley's professional playing career in the WNBA left an indelible mark on the league and the sport of basketball. Her achievements, leadership, and advocacy efforts continue to inspire and influence future generations.

Honors and Recognition

Dawn's contributions to the WNBA have been widely recognized. She has been inducted into various halls of fame, including the Women's Basketball Hall of Fame and the Naismith Memorial Basketball Hall of Fame. These honors are a testament to her impact on the sport and her enduring legacy.

Influence on Future Generations

Dawn's influence extends beyond her playing days. Her work as a coach and mentor continues to shape the future of women's basketball. She remains a role model and inspiration to young athletes, demonstrating that hard work, dedication, and leadership can lead to extraordinary achievements.

Conclusion

Dawn Staley's WNBA career is a story of excellence, leadership, and impact. From her early days with the Charlotte Sting to her time with the Houston Comets, Dawn consistently demonstrated her exceptional talent and leadership. Her contributions to the league and the sport of women's basketball are profound and enduring. Dawn's legacy as a player, leader, and advocate continues to inspire and influence, ensuring that her impact on the game will be felt for generations to come.

CHAPTER 7

TRANSITION TO COACHING

Early Coaching Experiences and Challenges

Dawn Staley's transition from a stellar playing career to a highly successful coaching career is a testament to her profound understanding of the game, leadership abilities, and relentless work ethic. Her journey into coaching began while she was still playing, and her early experiences and challenges shaped her into one of the most respected coaches in women's basketball.

This comprehensive exploration delves into her early coaching experiences, the challenges she faced, and the foundation she built for her legendary coaching career.

The Genesis of a Coaching Career

Dawn Staley's coaching career began unexpectedly early. While still a dominant player in the WNBA, she took on the role of head coach at Temple University in 2000. Balancing her responsibilities as a player and a coach required extraordinary dedication and time management, and it showcased her passion for teaching and leading.

Dual Roles: Player and Coach

In 2000, when Dawn accepted the head

coaching position at Temple University, she was still in the prime of her playing career with the Charlotte Sting in the WNBA. Taking on a dual role was unprecedented and highlighted her exceptional drive and ability to multitask. It was a testament to her commitment to the game and her desire to make an impact both on and off the court.

Building a Program at Temple

Temple University, located in Philadelphia, was not traditionally known as a powerhouse in women's basketball. Dawn faced the challenge of building a competitive program from the ground up. Her first task was to change the culture and mindset of the team, instilling a belief in winning and hard work.

Early Challenges and Learning Experiences
The initial phase of Dawn's coaching career

was fraught with challenges. From recruiting talented players to establishing a winning culture, Dawn had to navigate numerous obstacles. These early experiences were crucial in shaping her coaching philosophy and strategies.

Recruiting Challenges

One of the first challenges Dawn faced was recruiting. Attracting top talent to a program without a strong basketball tradition was difficult. Dawn had to rely on her reputation and vision for the program to persuade recruits to join Temple. Her ability to connect with young athletes and sell them on the potential for success under her guidance was key to her early recruiting efforts.

Establishing Credibility

As a new coach, establishing credibility with her players and peers was essential. While her playing career provided her with a high level of respect, coaching required a different skill set. Dawn had to prove herself as a capable and knowledgeable coach, earning the trust and confidence of her players and assistant coaches.

Balancing Coaching and Playing

Balancing her coaching responsibilities with her playing career was one of the most significant challenges Dawn faced. She had to manage her time meticulously, often flying from WNBA games to Temple practices and vice versa. This balancing act required immense physical and mental stamina, as well as a deep passion for the game. Despite the challenges, Dawn excelled in both roles, setting a standard of excellence and dedication.

Developing a Coaching Philosophy

Through her early experiences, Dawn began to develop a distinct coaching philosophy. Her approach to coaching was heavily influenced by her playing career and the coaches she had worked with. Her philosophy emphasized discipline, hard work, and a team-first mentality.

Emphasis on Defense

Dawn's playing career was marked by her defensive prowess, and this focus carried over into her coaching philosophy. She believed that a strong defensive foundation was critical to a team's success. At Temple, she instilled a defensive mindset, emphasizing the importance of effort, communication, and tenacity on the defensive end of the floor.

Player Development

Dawn was committed to developing her

players both on and off the court. She focused on improving their skills, basketball IQ, and understanding of the game. Additionally, she emphasized the importance of academic success and personal growth, preparing her players for life beyond basketball.

Building Team Chemistry

Dawn understood the importance of team chemistry and unity. She fostered a positive and inclusive team environment, where every player felt valued and motivated. Her leadership and ability to connect with her players were instrumental in building a cohesive and supportive team culture.

Achievements at Temple University

Despite the initial challenges, Dawn's tenure at Temple was marked by significant achievements and milestones. She transformed the program into a competitive force in women's college basketball.

Winning Seasons and Championships

Under Dawn's leadership, Temple enjoyed numerous winning seasons and conference championships. Her ability to turn around a struggling program was remarkable, and she quickly established Temple as a contender in the Atlantic 10 Conference. The team's success on the court was a reflection of Dawn's coaching acumen and her players' dedication.

NCAA Tournament Appearances

Dawn led Temple to several NCAA Tournament appearances, a significant accomplishment for the program. Competing on the national stage brought greater visibility to Temple's women's basketball and attracted more talented recruits. Dawn's success in the NCAA Tournament showcased her ability to prepare and lead her team in high-stakes situations.

Individual Player Success

Many of Dawn's players at Temple achieved individual success, earning conference honors and accolades. Her commitment to player development helped her athletes reach their full potential, both during their college careers and beyond. Several of her players went on to play professionally, further testament to her impact as a coach.

Transition to the University of South Carolina

In 2008, Dawn Staley took on a new challenge, becoming the head coach of the University of South Carolina women's basketball team. This move marked a significant step in her coaching career, providing her with an opportunity to build a powerhouse program in one of the most competitive conferences in college basketball.

Rebuilding the Program

When Dawn arrived at South Carolina, the program was in need of a rebuild. Her task was to elevate the team to national prominence, a challenge she embraced with enthusiasm. Her vision, work ethic, and recruiting prowess were instrumental in transforming South Carolina into a dominant force in women's basketball.

Recruiting Success

Dawn's ability to recruit top talent was evident from the start. She secured commitments from highly touted recruits, building a roster capable of competing with the best teams in the country. Her success on the recruiting trail was a result of her reputation, charisma, and the winning culture she was building at South Carolina.

Challenges and Triumphs at South Carolina

Dawn's journey at South Carolina was filled with challenges and triumphs. Building a championship-caliber program required patience, perseverance, and relentless effort. Her ability to navigate these challenges and achieve success solidified her status as one of the top coaches in women's basketball.

Establishing a Winning Culture

One of Dawn's first tasks at South Carolina was to establish a winning culture. This involved changing the mindset of her players and instilling a belief in their ability to succeed. Dawn's emphasis on hard work, discipline, and team unity was central to building a culture of excellence.

Competing in the SEC

The Southeastern Conference (SEC) is one of the toughest conferences in college basketball. Competing against traditional powerhouses like Tennessee and LSU posed significant challenges. Dawn's strategic acumen, preparation, and ability to motivate her players were key factors in South Carolina's success in the SEC.

Achieving Milestones

Dawn's tenure at South Carolina has been marked by numerous milestones and achievements. Under her leadership, the team has won multiple SEC championships, reached the Final Four, and secured a national championship. These accomplishments are a testament to Dawn's coaching abilities and the dedication of her players.

Leadership and Impact

Dawn Staley's impact as a coach goes beyond wins and championships. Her leadership, mentorship, and advocacy for women's sports have left a lasting legacy in the world of basketball.

Mentorship and Player Development

Dawn's commitment to mentoring her players and helping them develop both on and off the court is a hallmark of her coaching career. She takes a personal interest in her players' growth, providing guidance and support in all aspects of their lives. Her ability to connect with her players and inspire them to reach their full potential is a key factor in her success as a coach.

Advocacy for Women's Sports

Dawn has been a vocal advocate for women's sports throughout her career. She uses her platform to push for greater recognition and support for female athletes. Her advocacy efforts have contributed to the growth and development of women's basketball and have inspired countless young athletes.

Legacy and Influence

Dawn Staley's legacy as a coach is defined by her impact on the game and the lives of her players. Her success on the court, commitment to player development, and advocacy for women's sports have made her a trailblazer in the world of basketball. Her influence extends beyond her own teams, as she continues to inspire and shape the future of the sport.

Conclusion

Dawn Staley's transition to coaching was marked by early challenges and significant achievements. Her ability to navigate the complexities of coaching while maintaining her playing career is a testament to her dedication and passion for the game. From her early experiences at Temple University to her success at the University of South Carolina, Dawn's journey is a story of perseverance, leadership, and impact.

Her legacy as a coach is defined by her contributions to the sport, her mentorship of young athletes, and her advocacy for women's sports. Dawn Staley's coaching career continues to inspire and influence, ensuring that her impact on the game will be felt for generations to come.

CHAPTER 8

BUILDING A COACHING LEGACY

Leadership at Temple University and Beyond

Dawn Staley's coaching career is a testament to her ability to inspire, lead, and transform basketball programs into champions. From her initial foray into coaching at Temple University to her current role at the University of South Carolina, Staley has built a legacy of excellence, resilience, and leadership.

This in-depth exploration delves into her journey, highlighting the milestones, challenges, and strategies that have defined her coaching career and established her as one of the most influential figures in women's basketball.

The Genesis of a Coaching Career at Temple University

Dawn Staley's transition to coaching began while she was still an active player, a testament to her multifaceted talent and passion for the game. In 2000, Staley was appointed as the head coach of the Temple University women's basketball team, marking the beginning of an illustrious coaching career.

Accepting the Challenge

Taking the reins of the Temple Owls was a bold move. Temple's women's basketball program was not historically known as a powerhouse, and the task of building a competitive team from the ground up was formidable. Staley's acceptance of the position while still playing professionally in the WNBA with the Charlotte Sting demonstrated her commitment and ambitious vision.

Dual Roles: Player and Coach

Balancing the dual roles of player and coach required exceptional time management and dedication. Staley's schedule was grueling, often involving travel between WNBA games and Temple practices. Despite the challenges, she managed to excel in both roles, setting a high standard for her players and demonstrating her extraordinary work ethic.

Establishing a Winning Culture at Temple

Dawn Staley's impact on Temple University was immediate and profound. Her approach to coaching emphasized discipline, hard work, and a winning mentality. She was determined to change the culture of the program and instill a belief in success.

Building the Foundation

Staley's first task was to build a strong foundation for the program. This involved recruiting talented players who were committed to her vision. She focused on identifying athletes who possessed not only skill but also the character and work ethic necessary to thrive in her system. Her reputation as a player and leader helped attract recruits who were eager to learn from one of the best.

Implementing a Defensive Mindset

Defense was a cornerstone of Staley's

coaching philosophy. She believed that a strong defensive foundation was critical to a team's success. Under her leadership, Temple became known for its tenacious defense, which often stifled opponents and created opportunities for transition offense. This defensive mindset was instilled in every player, emphasizing effort, communication, and a relentless pursuit of excellence.

Achievements and Milestones at Temple

Staley's tenure at Temple was marked by significant achievements and milestones that transformed the program into a competitive force in women's college basketball.

Winning Seasons

Under Staley's leadership, Temple enjoyed numerous winning seasons. Her ability to turn around a struggling program was remarkable, and she quickly established the Owls as a contender in the Atlantic 10 Conference. The team's success on the court was a reflection of Staley's coaching acumen and her players' dedication.

Conference Championships

One of the most significant achievements during Staley's tenure at Temple was the team's success in winning conference championships. These victories were a testament to the hard work and resilience of the players and the effectiveness of Staley's coaching strategies. Winning conference titles brought greater visibility to the program and attracted more talented recruits.

NCAA Tournament Appearances

Staley led Temple to several NCAA Tournament appearances, a significant accomplishment for the program. Competing on the national stage brought greater visibility to Temple's women's basketball and attracted more talented recruits. Staley's success in the NCAA Tournament showcased her ability to prepare and lead her team in high-stakes situations.

Developing a Coaching Philosophy

Through her experiences at Temple, Dawn Staley developed a distinct coaching philosophy that emphasized discipline, hard work, and a team-first mentality. Her approach to coaching was heavily influenced by her playing career and the mentors she had along the way.

Emphasis on Player Development

Staley was committed to developing her

players both on and off the court. She focused on improving their skills, basketball IQ, and understanding of the game. Additionally, she emphasized the importance of academic success and personal growth, preparing her players for life beyond basketball. Her holistic approach to player development was a key factor in the success of her teams.

Leadership and Mentorship

Leadership was a hallmark of Staley's coaching style. She led by example, demonstrating a tireless work ethic and a commitment to excellence. Her ability to connect with her players on a personal level and inspire them to reach their full potential was a critical aspect of her success as a coach. Staley's mentorship extended beyond basketball, as she helped her players navigate the challenges of life and grow as individuals.

Strategic Acumen

Staley's strategic acumen was evident in her ability to outmaneuver opponents and make crucial adjustments during games. Her deep understanding of the game, combined with her ability to read situations and make quick decisions, made her an exceptional tactician. This strategic mindset was a significant advantage for her teams and contributed to their success on the court.

Transition to the University of South Carolina

In 2008, Dawn Staley took on a new challenge by becoming the head coach of the University of South Carolina women's basketball team. This move marked a significant step in her coaching career, providing her with an opportunity to build a powerhouse program in one of the most competitive conferences in college basketball.

Rebuilding the Program

When Staley arrived at South Carolina, the program was in need of a rebuild. Her task was to elevate the team to national prominence, a challenge she embraced with enthusiasm. Her vision, work ethic, and recruiting prowess were instrumental in transforming South Carolina into a dominant force in women's basketball.

Recruiting Success

Staley's ability to recruit top talent was evident from the start. She secured commitments from highly touted recruits, building a roster capable of competing with the best teams in the country. Her success on the recruiting trail was a result of her reputation, charisma, and the winning culture she was building at South Carolina.

Challenges and Triumphs at South Carolina

Dawn Staley's journey at South Carolina was filled with challenges and triumphs. Building a championship-caliber program required patience, perseverance, and relentless effort. Her ability to navigate these challenges and achieve success solidified her status as one of the top coaches in women's basketball.

Establishing a Winning Culture

One of Staley's first tasks at South Carolina was to establish a winning culture. This involved changing the mindset of her players and instilling a belief in their ability to succeed. Staley's emphasis on hard work, discipline, and team unity was central to building a culture of excellence.

Competing in the SEC

The Southeastern Conference (SEC) is one of the toughest conferences in college basketball. Competing against traditional powerhouses like Tennessee and LSU posed significant challenges. Staley's strategic acumen, preparation, and ability to motivate her players were key factors in South Carolina's success in the SEC.

Achieving Milestones

Staley's tenure at South Carolina has been marked by numerous milestones and achievements. Under her leadership, the team has won multiple SEC championships, reached the Final Four, and secured a national championship. These accomplishments are a testament to Staley's coaching abilities and the dedication of her players.

Leadership and Impact

Dawn Staley's impact as a coach goes beyond wins and championships. Her leadership, mentorship, and advocacy for women's sports have left a lasting legacy in the world of basketball.

Mentorship and Player Development

Staley's commitment to mentoring her players and helping them develop both on and off the court is a hallmark of her coaching career. She takes a personal interest in her players' growth, providing guidance and support in all aspects of their lives. Her ability to connect with her players and inspire them to reach their full potential is a key factor in her success as a coach.

Advocacy for Women's Sports

Staley has been a vocal advocate for

women's sports throughout her career. She uses her platform to push for greater recognition and support for female athletes. Her advocacy efforts have contributed to the growth and development of women's basketball and have inspired countless young athletes.

Legacy and Influence

Dawn Staley's legacy as a coach is defined by her impact on the game and the lives of her players. Her success on the court, commitment to player development, and advocacy for women's sports have made her a trailblazer in the world of basketball. Her influence extends beyond her own teams, as she continues to inspire and shape the future of the sport.

Building a Championship Program at South Carolina

Dawn Staley's tenure at South Carolina is

characterized by the transformation of the program into a national powerhouse. Her ability to build a championship-caliber team and sustain success is a testament to her coaching brilliance and leadership.

Recruitment of Top Talent

Recruiting top talent was a cornerstone of Staley's strategy at South Carolina. Her ability to identify and attract elite players was instrumental in building a competitive roster. Staley's reputation as a successful player and coach, combined with her vision for the program, made South Carolina an attractive destination for high school stars.

Development of a Winning Culture

Establishing a winning culture was essential to South Carolina's success. Staley emphasized discipline, hard work, and a team-first mentality. She created an environment where players were motivated to excel and support each other. This culture of excellence was reflected in the team's performance on the court.

Tactical Excellence

Staley's tactical excellence was evident in her ability to adapt and outmaneuver opponents. Her strategic adjustments during games and her preparation for different opponents were critical to the team's success. Staley's deep understanding of the game and her ability to make quick, effective decisions set her apart as a top coach.

Achieving National Prominence

Under Dawn Staley's leadership, the South Carolina women's basketball program ascended to national prominence, marked by significant milestones and remarkable achievements.

SEC Dominance

One of the key indicators of South Carolina's rise to prominence was their dominance in the Southeastern Conference (SEC). Competing in one of the toughest conferences in college basketball, South Carolina consistently finished at the top, winning multiple SEC regular-season and tournament championships. Staley's teams became known for their tenacious defense, fast-paced offense, and overall physical and mental toughness.

Final Four Appearances

Staley's strategic acumen and ability to prepare her team for high-stakes games were crucial in guiding South Carolina to several Final Four appearances. These deep runs in the NCAA Tournament showcased her ability to lead her team through the pressures of March Madness, where every game is a test of skill, strategy, and resilience.

National Championships

The pinnacle of Staley's coaching career at South Carolina came with winning the NCAA national championship. These victories were a culmination of years of hard work, strategic planning, and the relentless pursuit of excellence. Winning a national title solidified South Carolina's status as a powerhouse in women's college basketball and cemented Staley's legacy as one of the greatest coaches in the sport.

Player Development and Success

Dawn Staley's commitment to player development has been a cornerstone of her coaching philosophy. Her ability to nurture and develop talent has led to numerous individual successes and has greatly contributed to the overall success of her teams.

All-Americans and Award Winners

Under Staley's guidance, many players have achieved individual accolades, including All-American honors and national awards. Her ability to develop players' skills, basketball IQ, and overall understanding of the game has helped them reach their full potential. These individual successes have brought greater visibility and prestige to the South Carolina program.

Professional Careers

Many of Staley's players have gone on to have successful professional careers in the WNBA and overseas. Her emphasis on preparing her players for the next level has made South Carolina a destination for recruits who aspire to play professionally. Staley's own experience as a professional player has given her unique insights into what it takes to succeed at the highest levels of the sport.

Leadership and Mentorship

Dawn Staley's impact as a coach extends beyond the basketball court. Her leadership and mentorship have had a profound influence on her players, colleagues, and the broader basketball community.

Empowering Players

Staley's coaching style empowers her players to take ownership of their development and performance. She fosters an environment where players are encouraged to lead, make decisions, and hold themselves and their teammates accountable. This empowerment helps build confidence and leadership skills that serve her players well both on and off the court.

Advocacy for Women's Sports

Staley has been a tireless advocate for women's sports. She uses her platform to push for greater recognition, resources, and opportunities for female athletes. Her advocacy efforts have contributed to the growth and development of women's basketball and have inspired countless young athletes to pursue their dreams.

Role Model and Trailblazer

As one of the most successful and visible coaches in women's basketball, Staley serves as a role model and trailblazer for aspiring coaches and athletes. Her success has paved the way for more women to enter coaching and leadership roles in sports. Staley's journey, marked by perseverance, excellence, and a commitment to making a difference, inspires many.

Challenges and Triumphs Beyond South Carolina

Dawn Staley's coaching legacy extends beyond her tenure at South Carolina, encompassing her contributions to USA Basketball and her ongoing influence in the basketball community.

Coaching Team USA

Staley's coaching prowess was recognized on the international stage when she was appointed head coach of the USA women's national basketball team. Leading Team USA to gold medals in the Olympics and other international competitions has further solidified her reputation as one of the best coaches in the world. Her ability to manage and lead a team of elite athletes from various backgrounds and playing styles showcases her exceptional coaching skills.

Overcoming Challenges

Throughout her coaching career, Staley has faced numerous challenges, from rebuilding programs to competing against the best teams in the world. Her resilience and ability to overcome these challenges have been key to her success. Staley's journey is a testament to the importance of perseverance, adaptability, and a relentless pursuit of excellence.

Continuing to Inspire

Staley's influence continues to grow as she inspires the next generation of coaches and players. Her commitment to the game, her players, and the broader basketball community serves as a powerful example of what can be achieved with hard work, dedication, and a passion for excellence.

Legacy and Impact

Dawn Staley's legacy as a coach is defined by her impact on the game of basketball and the lives of her players. Her contributions to the sport extend beyond wins and championships, encompassing her role as a leader, mentor, and advocate.

Transforming Programs
Staley's ability to transform basketball programs into champions is a significant part of her legacy. Her success at Temple and South Carolina demonstrates her talent for building winning cultures and developing competitive teams. Her influence has left a lasting impact on these programs, setting a standard of excellence that will endure.

Mentorship and Player Development
Staley's commitment to mentoring and

developing her players is another crucial aspect of her legacy. She has helped countless young women grow as athletes and individuals, providing them with the skills and confidence to succeed both on and off the court. Her holistic approach to coaching has left a lasting impact on the lives of her players.

Advocacy for Women's Sports

Staley's advocacy for women's sports has had a profound influence on the growth and development of women's basketball. Her efforts to push for greater recognition, resources, and opportunities have helped elevate the sport and inspire future generations of female athletes. Staley's voice and actions have contributed to the broader movement for gender equality in sports.

Trailblazer and Role Model

As a trailblazer in the world of women's

basketball, Staley serves as a role model for aspiring coaches and athletes. Her journey, marked by perseverance, excellence, and a commitment to making a difference, inspires many. Staley's success has paved the way for more women to enter coaching and leadership roles in sports, creating a lasting impact on the future of the game.

Conclusion

Dawn Staley's coaching career is a testament to her leadership, resilience, and unwavering commitment to excellence. From her early days at Temple University to her current role at the University of South Carolina and beyond, Staley has built a legacy that extends far beyond wins and championships. Her impact on the game of basketball, her players, and the broader sports community is profound and enduring.

Staley's ability to transform programs, develop talent, and advocate for women's sports has made her one of the most influential figures in women's basketball. Her leadership and mentorship have inspired countless young athletes and coaches, paving the way for future generations. As a trailblazer and role model, Staley's journey continues to inspire and shape the future of the sport.

The legacy of Dawn Staley is one of excellence, resilience, and impact. Her contributions to basketball and her influence on the lives of her players will be felt for generations to come. As she continues to lead and inspire, Staley's legacy as one of the greatest coaches in the history of women's basketball is firmly established.

CHAPTER 9

NATIONAL TEAM COACHING

Guiding Team USA to Success on the International Stage

the profession. Staley's approachability and openness have made her a respected figure among her peers, and her commitment to mentoring future coaches has had a profound impact on the growth and development of women's basketball.

Advocacy for Gender Equality in Sports

Highlighting Disparities

Staley has been a vocal advocate for gender equality in sports, using her platform to highlight the disparities in resources, recognition, and opportunities between men's and women's sports. Her efforts have brought attention to issues such as pay equity, media coverage, and investment in women's sports. Staley's advocacy has been instrumental in pushing for change, leading to increased support and visibility for women's basketball.

Pushing for Change

Staley's advocacy goes beyond raising awareness; she actively pushes for tangible changes that benefit female athletes. Whether it's lobbying for better facilities, more equitable funding, or greater representation in coaching and administrative positions, Staley's efforts have helped create a more level playing field. Her dedication to promoting gender equality has made her a leading voice in the broader movement for equity in sports.

Strategic Leadership on the International Stage

Adapting to the Competition

One of the key challenges in international basketball is the need to adapt to different playing styles and strategies used by teams from around the world. Staley's experience and strategic acumen have been crucial in preparing Team USA to face a diverse range of opponents. She meticulously studies the strengths and weaknesses of rival teams, developing game plans that exploit their vulnerabilities while maximizing Team USA's advantages.

In-Game Adjustments

Staley's ability to make effective in-game adjustments has been a critical factor in Team USA's success. She has a keen sense for recognizing when changes are needed, whether it's altering defensive schemes, adjusting offensive sets, or managing player rotations. Her quick thinking and strategic insights allow Team USA to stay one step ahead of their opponents, maintaining control of the game and responding effectively to challenges as they arise.

Motivating Elite Athletes

Coaching a team of elite athletes requires a unique approach to motivation and leadership. Staley's ability to connect with her players on a personal level, understand their individual motivations, and inspire them to perform at their best is a hallmark of her coaching style. She creates an environment where players feel valued and motivated, fostering a culture of excellence and mutual support that drives the team to achieve its goals.

Key Tournament Performances

2018 FIBA Women's Basketball World Cup

The 2018 FIBA Women's Basketball World Cup was a defining moment in Staley's coaching career. Under her leadership, Team USA demonstrated their dominance on the international stage, securing the gold medal with a series of impressive performances. Staley's strategic planning and ability to motivate her players were evident throughout the tournament, as

Team USA navigated the challenges of international competition with poise and precision.

Group Stage Success

Team USA's group stage performance set the tone for the tournament. They secured decisive victories against Senegal, China, and Latvia, showcasing their offensive prowess and defensive discipline. Staley's emphasis on preparation and adaptability was evident in the team's ability to execute their game plans effectively, dominating their opponents and building momentum for the knockout stages.

Navigating the Knockout Stages

In the knockout stages, Team USA faced tougher competition but continued to excel. They defeated Nigeria and Belgium with commanding performances, demonstrating their tactical versatility and depth. Staley's in-game adjustments and ability to keep her players focused and motivated were critical in these high-stakes matches, allowing Team USA to maintain their high level of performance.

Gold Medal Match

The gold medal match against Australia was a showcase of Staley's strategic brilliance. Team USA executed a disciplined defensive strategy and utilized their size advantage to control the game, securing a 73-56 victory. This triumph was a testament to Staley's leadership and tactical acumen, reinforcing her reputation as one of the top coaches in the world.

2020 Tokyo Olympics

The 2020 Tokyo Olympics, held in 2021 due to the COVID-19 pandemic, presented unique challenges for Staley and Team USA.

Despite the disruptions caused by the pandemic, Staley's leadership and strategic planning were crucial in guiding the team to another gold medal.

Overcoming Pandemic Challenges

The pandemic presented significant challenges, including disruptions to training and preparation, health and safety concerns, and the need to navigate a rapidly changing landscape. Staley's ability to maintain team cohesion and focus during this period was crucial. Her adaptability and resilience were key factors in ensuring that Team USA was well-prepared and motivated to compete at the highest level.

Group Stage Dominance

Team USA's group stage performance was marked by impressive victories against Nigeria, Japan, and France. Staley's strategic rotations and emphasis on defensive discipline were evident as the team executed their game plans with precision. The ability to adjust to different playing styles and maintain a high level of performance under pressure was a testament to Staley's coaching prowess.

Navigating the Knockout Stages

In the knockout stages, Team USA faced formidable opponents but continued to demonstrate their dominance. Victories against Australia and Serbia highlighted the team's tactical versatility and depth. Staley's in-game adjustments and ability to motivate her players were critical in these high-stakes matches, allowing Team USA to maintain their high level of performance and secure a place in the gold medal match.

Gold Medal Triumph

The gold medal match against Japan was a showcase of Team USA's defensive discipline and strategic execution. Staley's game plan, which focused on neutralizing Japan's speed and precision, proved effective as Team USA secured a 90-75 victory. This triumph marked another gold medal for Team USA and further solidified Staley's legacy as a premier coach in women's basketball.

Legacy and Impact on International Basketball

Elevating Team USA

Under Staley's leadership, Team USA has continued to set the standard for excellence in women's basketball. Her strategic innovations, emphasis on team culture, and ability to motivate elite athletes have been key factors in maintaining the team's dominance on the international stage. Staley's contributions have not only led to continued success for Team USA but have also elevated the profile of women's basketball globally.

Inspiring Future Generations

Staley's success as a coach and leader has

inspired countless young athletes and coaches around the world. Her journey, marked by perseverance, excellence, and a commitment to making a difference, serves as a powerful example of what can be achieved with hard work and dedication. Staley's influence extends beyond the basketball court, inspiring future generations to pursue their dreams and make a positive impact in their communities.

Advocating for Women's Sports

Staley has been a tireless advocate for women's sports, using her platform to push for greater recognition, resources, and opportunities for female athletes. Her advocacy efforts have contributed to the growth and development of women's basketball, helping to create a more equitable and supportive environment for future generations of players. Staley's dedication to promoting gender equality in sports has made her a leading voice in the broader movement for equity and inclusion.

Building a Coaching Legacy

Staley's impact on the coaching profession is profound and enduring. Her success at both the collegiate and international levels has set a new standard for excellence in coaching. Staley's emphasis on player development, strategic innovation, and fostering a strong team culture has influenced coaching practices across the sport. Her legacy as a mentor and advocate for women in coaching continues to inspire and empower the next generation of leaders in basketball.

Conclusion

Dawn Staley's journey as the head coach of the USA women's national basketball team is a testament to her exceptional leadership, strategic acumen, and unwavering commitment to excellence. Her ability to guide Team USA to success on the international stage, overcoming numerous challenges and achieving remarkable victories, has solidified her status as one of the greatest coaches in the history of women's basketball.

Staley's impact extends beyond the court, encompassing her role as a mentor, advocate, and trailblazer. Her contributions to the growth and development of women's basketball, her dedication to promoting gender equality in sports, and her influence on the next generation of coaches and players are profound and enduring.

As she continues to lead and inspire, Dawn Staley's legacy as a premier coach and influential figure in the world of basketball is firmly established, shaping the future of the sport for generations to come.

CHAPTER 10

OFF THE COURT

Philanthropy, Community Involvement, and Personal Life

Dawn Staley's impact extends far beyond her achievements on the basketball court. Her dedication to philanthropy, community involvement, and personal growth has made her a respected and influential figure both within and outside the sports world.

This exploration delves into Staley's off-court endeavors, highlighting her charitable work, community engagement, and personal life, offering a comprehensive view of the woman behind the coaching legend.

Philanthropy and Charitable Initiatives

The Dawn Staley Foundation

In 1996, Dawn Staley founded the Dawn Staley Foundation, an organization dedicated to empowering young people through sports and education. The foundation's mission is to create opportunities for at-risk youth in underserved communities, providing them with the tools and resources necessary to succeed both academically and athletically.

Mentorship and Leadership Programs

One of the cornerstone initiatives of the Dawn Staley Foundation is its mentorship and leadership programs. These programs aim to instill confidence, discipline, and a sense of responsibility in young participants. By pairing young people with mentors, the foundation helps them develop critical life skills and provides guidance and support as they navigate the challenges of growing up in underserved communities.

Academic Support

The foundation places a strong emphasis on education, offering tutoring, scholarship programs, and college preparation workshops. Staley understands the importance of academic success in providing opportunities for the future, and her foundation works tirelessly to ensure that young people have access to the resources and support they need to excel in their studies.

Sports and Recreational Activities

Recognizing the power of sports to teach valuable life lessons and build character, the Dawn Staley Foundation organizes sports camps, clinics, and recreational activities. These programs not only promote physical fitness but also teach teamwork, perseverance, and the importance of hard work. By engaging young people in positive activities, the foundation helps keep them off the streets and focused on their goals.

Support for Breast Cancer Research

Staley's philanthropic efforts also extend to health-related causes. She has been an active supporter of breast cancer research and awareness, participating in fundraising events and campaigns to support organizations dedicated to finding a cure. Staley's involvement in these efforts is deeply personal, as she has seen the impact of breast cancer on friends and family members. Her commitment to raising awareness and funds for research highlights her dedication to making a difference in the lives of those affected by the disease.

Advocacy for Equality and Social Justice

Staley is a passionate advocate for equality and social justice, using her platform to speak out on issues such as racial inequality, gender discrimination, and social injustice. She has participated in numerous campaigns and initiatives aimed at promoting equality and fostering a more inclusive society. Staley's advocacy work includes speaking engagements, public statements, and partnerships with organizations dedicated to advancing social justice.

Black Lives Matter Movement

In the wake of the Black Lives Matter movement, Staley has been an outspoken advocate for racial equality and justice. She has used her platform to raise awareness about systemic racism and to call for meaningful change. Staley's involvement in the movement includes participating in protests, delivering powerful speeches, and collaborating with other athletes and public figures to promote social justice initiatives.

Gender Equality in Sports

Staley's advocacy for gender equality extends to her work in sports. She has been a vocal proponent of equal pay, better resources, and increased visibility for female athletes. Staley's efforts have helped bring attention to the disparities that exist in sports and have contributed to the ongoing push for greater equity and representation for women in athletics.

Community Involvement

Engagement with Local Communities

Staley is deeply committed to giving back to the communities that have supported her throughout her career. She regularly engages with local communities, participating in events, visiting schools, and supporting local initiatives. Staley's presence and involvement in these communities serve as a source of inspiration and motivation for young people, showing them that success is possible through hard work and dedication.

School Visits and Educational Programs

One of Staley's favorite ways to engage with local communities is through school visits and educational programs. She frequently visits schools to speak with students, sharing her story and offering words of encouragement. Staley's visits often include motivational talks, Q&A sessions, and interactive activities designed to inspire students to pursue their dreams and work hard in their studies.

Community Sports Clinics

Staley's passion for basketball and commitment to youth development are evident in her involvement in community sports clinics. She regularly hosts and participates in clinics that provide young athletes with the opportunity to learn from one of the best in the game. These clinics not only teach basketball skills but also emphasize the importance of discipline, teamwork, and perseverance.

Support for Local Charities

In addition to her own foundation, Staley supports a variety of local charities and non-profit organizations. She participates in fundraising events, donates her time and resources, and uses her platform to raise awareness for causes she cares about.

Staley's involvement with local charities reflects her commitment to making a positive impact on the communities she serves.

Food Drives and Homeless Shelters

Staley has been involved in food drives and efforts to support homeless shelters, recognizing the importance of addressing basic needs in her community. She has partnered with local organizations to collect and distribute food, clothing, and other essential items to those in need. Staley's efforts in this area highlight her compassion and dedication to helping the most vulnerable members of society.

Personal Life and Values

Family and Relationships

Family is a central part of Dawn Staley's life,

and she often speaks about the influence her family has had on her values and career. Growing up in North Philadelphia, Staley was raised in a close-knit family that instilled in her the importance of hard work, perseverance, and giving back to the community.

Early Life and Influences

Staley's parents, Clarence and Estelle, were instrumental in shaping her character and work ethic. They emphasized the value of education and encouraged Staley to pursue her passions, including basketball. Her parents' support and guidance provided a strong foundation for her future success, and Staley often credits them with helping her achieve her goals.

Maintaining Close Family Ties

Despite her busy schedule, Staley makes it a priority to maintain close ties with her family. She frequently visits her family in Philadelphia and stays connected with her siblings and extended family members. Staley's commitment to family reflects her deep-rooted values and the importance she places on maintaining strong personal relationships.

Personal Growth and Development

Staley's journey has been marked by continuous personal growth and development. She is committed to learning and self-improvement, constantly seeking new ways to expand her knowledge and skills. This commitment to personal growth extends beyond her professional career and includes her efforts to better understand and address social issues.

Lifelong Learning

Staley's dedication to lifelong learning is evident in her pursuit of educational opportunities and her openness to new experiences. She regularly attends workshops, seminars, and conferences to stay informed about the latest developments in coaching, leadership, and social justice. Staley's commitment to learning ensures that she remains at the forefront of her field and continues to grow as a leader and advocate.

Personal Reflections and Self-Care

Amidst her many responsibilities, Staley recognizes the importance of self-care and personal reflection. She practices mindfulness and takes time to reflect on her experiences, learning from both her successes and challenges. Staley's focus on self-care helps her maintain balance and resilience, enabling her to continue making a positive impact in her professional and personal life.

Interests and Hobbies

Outside of basketball and her philanthropic efforts, Staley has a variety of interests and hobbies that contribute to her well-rounded character. These interests provide her with a sense of relaxation and fulfillment, helping her recharge and stay grounded.

Music and Arts

Staley has a deep appreciation for music and the arts. She enjoys attending concerts, visiting art galleries, and exploring different forms of creative expression. Her love for music and the arts provides a source of inspiration and allows her to connect with different aspects of culture and creativity.

Travel and Exploration

Travel is another passion of Staley's, and she enjoys exploring new places and experiencing different cultures. Whether it's visiting historical sites, trying new cuisines, or meeting people from diverse backgrounds, Staley's travels enrich her perspective and broaden her understanding of the world.

Reading and Writing

Staley is an avid reader and enjoys delving into a wide range of topics, from biographies and history to fiction and self-help. Reading provides her with new insights and ideas, fueling her passion for learning and growth. Additionally, Staley enjoys writing, often penning reflections on her experiences and thoughts on various topics. Writing serves as a creative outlet and a means of sharing her journey with others.

Impact and Legacy

Inspiring Future Generations

Dawn Staley's impact extends far beyond

her own achievements. Through her philanthropy, community involvement, and personal example, she has inspired countless young people to pursue their dreams and make a difference in their communities. Staley's legacy is not only defined by her success on the court but also by the lives she has touched and the positive change she has helped create.

Role Model and Mentor

Staley's role as a mentor and role model is one of the most significant aspects of her legacy. She has guided and supported many young athletes and coaches, helping them navigate the challenges of their careers and achieve their goals. Staley's mentorship has had a lasting impact on the development of women's basketball and has helped pave the way for future generations of leaders in the sport.

Advocate for Social Change

Staley's advocacy for social change has contributed to a broader movement for equality and justice. Her efforts to raise awareness and promote change in areas such as racial equality, gender discrimination, and health have made a meaningful impact on society. Staley's dedication to these causes highlights her commitment to using her platform for good and making a lasting difference in the world.

Staley continues her journey, her commitment to making a positive impact remains unwavering. She strives to broaden her influence, reaching new heights in her advocacy and community efforts.

Continuing to Make a Difference

Expansion of the Dawn Staley Foundation

Staley's vision for the future includes expanding the reach and impact of the Dawn Staley Foundation. Plans for growth involve increasing the number of mentorship programs, educational initiatives, and sports activities available to at-risk youth. By securing additional funding and building partnerships with other organizations, Staley aims to provide even more resources and opportunities for young people in underserved communities.

National and Global Outreach

Staley envisions the Dawn Staley Foundation extending its impact beyond Philadelphia, reaching youth across the nation and even globally. By developing online programs and resources, the foundation can offer mentorship, educational support, and sports training to young people regardless of their location. This expansion would allow the foundation to touch the lives of more young people, helping them achieve their full potential.

Collaboration with Other Organizations

Partnerships with other non-profits, educational institutions, and sports organizations are key to the foundation's growth. By collaborating with like-minded entities, the Dawn Staley Foundation can leverage additional expertise, resources, and networks to enhance its programs and services. These partnerships will enable the foundation to address a wider range of needs and make a more significant impact on the communities it serves.

Leadership in Advocacy and Social Justice

Staley remains deeply committed to her advocacy work, particularly in the areas of racial equality, gender discrimination, and social justice. She continues to use her voice to raise awareness, push for policy changes, and inspire others to join the fight for equality.

Speaking Engagements and Public Appearances

Staley frequently participates in speaking engagements and public appearances to discuss important social issues and share her experiences. Her powerful speeches and thoughtful insights have inspired many to take action and contribute to the fight for justice. Staley's ability to connect with diverse audiences and convey her message effectively makes her a highly sought-after speaker and advocate.

Campaigns and Initiatives

Staley's involvement in campaigns and initiatives aimed at promoting social justice continues to grow. She collaborates with various organizations to develop and implement programs that address systemic inequalities and provide support to marginalized communities. Whether it's through fundraising efforts, public awareness campaigns, or grassroots organizing, Staley is dedicated to creating meaningful change.

Personal Growth and Future Aspirations

Continuous Learning and Development

Staley's commitment to personal growth is a lifelong endeavor. She remains dedicated to expanding her knowledge and skills, seeking out new learning opportunities, and embracing new challenges. This commitment to self-improvement not only benefits her own development but also enhances her ability to lead and inspire others.

Pursuing Advanced Education

Staley has expressed interest in pursuing advanced education, potentially in areas such as leadership, social justice, or public administration. Furthering her education would provide her with additional tools and perspectives to enhance her advocacy and philanthropic efforts. Staley's pursuit of advanced education reflects her belief in the power of knowledge and her dedication to making a positive impact.

Exploring New Interests

Staley continues to explore new interests and hobbies, finding inspiration and fulfillment in different areas of life. Whether it's through travel, artistic pursuits, or new forms of creative expression, she remains open to new experiences that enrich her life and broaden her horizons. These explorations contribute to her personal growth and provide fresh perspectives that she can bring to her work.

Future Goals and Aspirations

Staley's future goals and aspirations are driven by her desire to continue making a difference and leaving a lasting legacy. She envisions a future where her foundation's impact is felt worldwide, where her advocacy efforts have contributed to meaningful social change, and where her personal growth has allowed her to reach new heights in her career and beyond.

Expanding Philanthropic Efforts

Staley aims to expand her philanthropic efforts, potentially establishing new initiatives or foundations that address additional social issues. By diversifying her philanthropic portfolio, she can tackle a broader range of challenges and make an even greater impact on the lives of those in need.

Inspiring the Next Generation

One of Staley's primary goals is to inspire the next generation of leaders, athletes, and advocates. She hopes to continue serving as a mentor and role model, guiding young people as they pursue their dreams and work to create positive change in their communities. Staley's legacy will be defined not only by her own achievements but also by the success and impact of those she has inspired.

Conclusion

Dawn Staley's contributions off the court are as impressive and impactful as her accomplishments in basketball. Her dedication to philanthropy, community involvement, and personal growth has made her a respected and influential figure in the sports world and beyond. Through her foundation, advocacy work, and personal example, Staley has touched countless lives and inspired a new generation of leaders and advocates.

Staley's journey is a testament to the power of perseverance, passion, and a commitment to making a difference. As she continues to expand her philanthropic efforts, advocate for social justice, and pursue personal growth, her legacy will only grow stronger. Dawn Staley's impact will be felt for generations to come, as she continues to inspire others to strive for excellence and make a positive impact on the world.

CHAPTER 11

IMPACT ON WOMEN'S BASKETBALL

Contributions to the Sport and Athlete Empowerment

Dawn Staley's influence on women's basketball is profound and multifaceted. From her remarkable career as a player to her transformative work as a coach and advocate, Staley has made significant contributions to the sport and has been a powerful force in empowering female athletes. This exploration delves into her contributions to women's basketball, her role in athlete empowerment, and the lasting legacy she is creating.

Contributions as a Player

Collegiate Career at the University of Virginia

Dawn Staley's collegiate career at the University of Virginia (UVA) set the stage for her future success and influence in women's basketball. During her time at UVA, Staley demonstrated exceptional skill, leadership, and determination, becoming one of the most celebrated players in college basketball history.

Record-Breaking Achievements

Staley's time at UVA was marked by numerous record-breaking achievements. She led the Cavaliers to three consecutive Final Four appearances from 1990 to 1992, solidifying her reputation as one of the top players in the nation. Staley's outstanding performance earned her multiple accolades, including two Naismith College Player of the Year awards and three Kodak All-American honors.

Leadership and Teamwork

Staley's leadership on the court was unparalleled. As the team's point guard, she was the floor general, orchestrating plays and setting the pace for the game. Her ability to inspire and elevate her teammates was evident in the Cavaliers' success during her tenure. Staley's leadership skills, honed during her collegiate career, would later become a hallmark of her coaching style.

Professional Playing Career

Staley's professional playing career further solidified her status as a basketball icon. She played in the American Basketball League

(ABL) and the Women's National Basketball Association (WNBA), where she continued to excel and inspire.

Success in the ABL and WNBA

In the ABL, Staley played for the Richmond Rage and the Philadelphia Rage, earning All-Star honors and leading her teams to success. When the ABL folded, Staley transitioned to the WNBA, where she played for the Charlotte Sting and the Houston Comets. During her time in the WNBA, Staley was a six-time All-Star and earned several All-WNBA Team selections. Her impact on the court was matched by her ability to mentor younger players and serve as a role model.

International Competitions

Staley's contributions to women's basketball extended to the international stage. She represented Team USA in multiple Olympic

Games, winning three gold medals (1996, 2000, and 2004). Her leadership and performance in international competitions helped elevate the profile of women's basketball and inspired a new generation of athletes.

Transition to Coaching

Early Coaching Experiences

Staley's transition from player to coach was seamless, and she quickly established herself as a formidable force in the coaching world. Her early coaching experiences laid the groundwork for her future success and impact on the sport.

Temple University

Staley began her coaching career at Temple University in 2000, while she was still playing in the WNBA. Under her leadership, the Temple Owls experienced a remarkable turnaround, earning multiple NCAA tournament appearances and winning several Atlantic 10 Conference titles. Staley's success at Temple demonstrated her ability to translate her on-court knowledge into effective coaching strategies.

Development of Coaching Philosophy

During her time at Temple, Staley developed a coaching philosophy centered on discipline, hard work, and player empowerment. She emphasized the importance of building strong relationships with her players and creating a supportive environment that fostered both personal and athletic growth. This philosophy would become a cornerstone of her coaching career.

Leadership at the University of South Carolina

Staley's move to the University of South Carolina in 2008 marked the beginning of a new chapter in her coaching career. As the head coach of the Gamecocks, Staley transformed the program into a national powerhouse, achieving unprecedented success.

Building a Championship Program

Under Staley's leadership, the Gamecocks won their first NCAA championship in 2017, followed by another championship in 2022. Her ability to recruit top talent, develop players, and implement effective game strategies has made South Carolina one of the most dominant programs in women's basketball. Staley's success at South Carolina has not only elevated the program but also increased the visibility and popularity of women's basketball.

Player Development and Empowerment

Staley's commitment to player development and empowerment is evident in the success of her athletes. She has coached numerous players who have gone on to have successful professional careers, including several WNBA stars. Staley's emphasis on education, personal growth, and leadership has prepared her players for success both on and off the court.

Advocate for Women's Basketball

Promoting Gender Equality

Staley has been a vocal advocate for gender equality in sports, using her platform to raise awareness about the disparities faced by female athletes. Her efforts have contributed to the ongoing push for equal resources, opportunities, and recognition for women in basketball.

Advocacy for Equal Pay

Staley has spoken out about the need for equal pay for female athletes, highlighting the significant pay gap between men's and women's sports. Her advocacy has helped bring attention to this issue and has inspired others to join the fight for fair compensation.

Visibility and Media Coverage

Staley has also worked to increase the visibility and media coverage of women's basketball. By promoting the achievements of female athletes and advocating for more coverage of women's sports, she has helped elevate the profile of women's basketball and attract new fans to the game.

Mentorship and Support for Female Coaches

Staley's impact extends beyond her players

to include her support for other female coaches. She has mentored numerous young coaches, providing guidance and support as they navigate their careers. Staley's efforts to empower and uplift female coaches have helped create a more inclusive and supportive environment within the coaching community.

Initiatives for Female Coaches

Staley has been involved in various initiatives aimed at supporting and developing female coaches. She has participated in workshops, conferences, and mentorship programs designed to provide female coaches with the tools and resources they need to succeed. Her commitment to supporting her peers has contributed to the growth and development of the coaching profession.

Breaking Barriers

Staley's success as a coach has helped break

barriers and pave the way for other women in the profession. Her achievements have demonstrated that women can excel in leadership roles in sports, challenging traditional gender norms and inspiring more women to pursue careers in coaching.

Legacy and Long-Term Impact

Lasting Influence on Players

One of Staley's most significant legacies is the lasting influence she has had on her players. Her commitment to their development, both as athletes and individuals, has left a profound impact on their lives.

Alumni Success Stories

Many of Staley's former players have gone on to achieve great success, both on and off the court. Their accomplishments serve as a testament to Staley's effective coaching and mentorship. The success stories of her alumni continue to inspire current and future players, showcasing the impact of Staley's guidance.

Lifelong Relationships

Staley has built lifelong relationships with many of her players, maintaining close connections even after they leave her program. These relationships are a reflection of the deep bond she forms with her athletes and her ongoing commitment to their success and well-being.

Contributions to the Growth of Women's Basketball

Staley's contributions to the growth of women's basketball are immeasurable. Through her success as a player and coach, her advocacy work, and her efforts to empower female athletes, she has helped elevate the sport to new heights.

Increasing Participation and Interest

Staley's influence has contributed to an increase in participation and interest in women's basketball. Her success and visibility have inspired countless young girls to pursue the sport, helping to grow the next generation of female basketball players.

Enhancing the Competitive Landscape

Staley's success at the University of South Carolina has raised the bar for competitiveness in women's basketball. Her ability to build a championship program has inspired other schools to invest in their women's basketball programs, contributing to a more competitive and exciting landscape for the sport.

Continuing to Inspire

Future Goals and Aspirations

Staley's journey is far from over, and she continues to set new goals and aspirations for herself and her teams. Her dedication to excellence and her desire to make a positive impact drive her to keep pushing forward.

Pursuit of More Championships

Staley remains focused on leading her teams to more championships and achieving new milestones. Her commitment to success on the court is matched by her dedication to developing her players and preparing them for life beyond basketball.

Expanding Her Influence

Staley aims to expand her influence beyond basketball, continuing her advocacy work and philanthropic efforts. By leveraging her platform and her reputation, she hopes to make an even greater impact on issues such as gender equality, social justice, and youth development.

Inspiring the Next Generation

Staley's legacy will be defined by the inspiration she provides to the next generation of athletes, coaches, and advocates. Her story serves as a powerful example of what can be achieved through hard work, determination, and a commitment to making a difference.

Role Model for Young Girls

Staley's journey from North Philadelphia to the pinnacle of women's basketball serves as a powerful role model for young girls. Her story shows that with dedication and perseverance, they too can achieve their dreams and make a significant impact in their chosen fields.

Mentor and Leader

As a mentor and leader, Staley continues to guide and inspire those around her. Her commitment to empowering others ensures that her impact will be felt for generations to come.

Conclusion

Dawn Staley's impact on women's basketball and athlete empowerment is vast and enduring. From her remarkable playing career to her transformative work as a coach and advocate, she has made significant contributions to the sport and has empowered countless female athletes. Her commitment to gender equality, her mentorship of young coaches, and her dedication to developing her players both on and off the court have cemented her legacy as a trailblazer in women's basketball.

As she continues to expand her philanthropic efforts, advocate for social justice, and pursue personal growth, Staley's legacy will only grow stronger. Her story is a testament to the power of perseverance, passion, and a commitment to making a difference. Dawn Staley's impact will be felt for generations to come, as she continues to inspire others to strive for excellence and make a positive impact on the world.

CHAPTER 12

ACHIEVEMENTS AND AWARDS

Career Highlights, Honors, and Records

Dawn Staley's illustrious career in basketball is a testament to her extraordinary talent, relentless work ethic, and unwavering commitment to excellence. Her journey from a standout player to a revered coach and influential leader in the world of sports is marked by numerous achievements and awards. This chapter delves into the career highlights, honors, and records that have defined Staley's remarkable legacy.

Early Career Highlights

High School Stardom

Dawn Staley's path to greatness began at Dobbins Technical High School in Philadelphia, where she quickly established herself as a basketball prodigy. Her high school career was filled with impressive accomplishments that laid the foundation for her future success.

Philadelphia Public League Championships

During her time at Dobbins Tech, Staley led her team to multiple Philadelphia Public League Championships. Her leadership and scoring prowess were instrumental in the team's dominance, and she earned recognition as one of the top high school players in the country. Staley's ability to perform under pressure and elevate her teammates foreshadowed her future success at the collegiate and professional levels.

High School All-American

Staley's exceptional performances earned her high school All-American honors, solidifying her status as one of the nation's premier players. Her skill set, characterized by her precise ball-handling, court vision, and scoring ability, drew the attention of college recruiters from across the country. Staley's high school achievements set the stage for a stellar collegiate career.

Collegiate Career at the University of Virginia

Dawn Staley's impact on women's basketball reached new heights during her time at the

University of Virginia (UVA). Her collegiate career is celebrated for its record-breaking achievements, leadership, and contributions to the growth of the sport.

Leading the Cavaliers to Success

Final Four Appearances

One of the most significant highlights of Staley's collegiate career was leading the UVA Cavaliers to three consecutive Final Four appearances in the NCAA Women's Basketball Tournament from 1990 to 1992. Staley's leadership on the court and her ability to deliver in clutch moments were pivotal in the Cavaliers' deep tournament runs. Her performances during these tournaments earned her widespread acclaim and established her as one of the best players in college basketball history.

Naismith College Player of the Year

Staley's dominance on the court was recognized with multiple individual accolades. She was awarded the prestigious Naismith College Player of the Year twice, in 1991 and 1992. This honor, given to the best player in college basketball, highlighted Staley's exceptional talent and impact on the game. Her ability to control the tempo, make critical plays, and lead her team to victory set her apart from her peers.

Kodak All-American Honors

In addition to the Naismith awards, Staley earned Kodak All-American honors three times during her collegiate career. This recognition further solidified her status as one of the top players in the nation. Staley's consistency, versatility, and ability to excel in all facets of the game made her a standout performer and a true leader on the court.

Career Records and Milestones

Scoring and Assists Records

Staley's time at UVA was marked by impressive statistical achievements. She set multiple school records, including career points and assists. Her ability to score from all areas of the court and her exceptional playmaking skills made her a dual threat that opponents struggled to contain. Staley's records at UVA remain a testament to her extraordinary talent and dedication.

Induction into the UVA Hall of Fame

In recognition of her outstanding contributions to the program, Staley was inducted into the University of Virginia Hall of Fame. This honor celebrated her impact on the school's basketball legacy and her role in elevating the program to national prominence. Staley's influence at UVA extended beyond her playing days, as she continued to inspire future generations of Cavaliers.

Professional Playing Career

Dawn Staley's professional playing career further solidified her status as a basketball legend. Her success in the American Basketball League (ABL) and the Women's National Basketball Association (WNBA) showcased her versatility, leadership, and ability to excel at the highest levels of competition.

American Basketball League (ABL)

Richmond Rage and Philadelphia Rage

Staley began her professional career in the

ABL, where she played for the Richmond Rage and later the Philadelphia Rage. Her impact on the league was immediate, as she earned All-Star honors and led her teams to success. Staley's ability to perform at an elite level in the ABL demonstrated her readiness for the global stage.

ABL All-Star and Leadership

Staley's time in the ABL was marked by her exceptional play and leadership. She was named to the ABL All-Star team, highlighting her status as one of the league's top players. Her ability to guide her team on the court and her influence in the locker room made her a valuable asset to her teams and a respected figure in the league.

Women's National Basketball Association (WNBA)

Charlotte Sting and Houston Comets

When the ABL folded, Staley transitioned to the WNBA, where she continued to shine. She played for the Charlotte Sting and later the Houston Comets, earning multiple All-Star selections and All-WNBA Team honors. Staley's success in the WNBA further cemented her legacy as one of the greatest players in women's basketball history.

WNBA All-Star and Milestones

Staley's WNBA career was filled with remarkable achievements. She was a six-time WNBA All-Star, showcasing her consistency and excellence over the years. Her ability to lead her teams and deliver standout performances earned her recognition as one of the league's premier players. Staley's impact on the court was matched by her contributions to the growth and popularity of the WNBA.

International Success

Dawn Staley's contributions to women's basketball extended to the international stage, where she represented Team USA in multiple Olympic Games and other international competitions. Her success with the national team added to her illustrious career and highlighted her status as a global basketball icon.

Olympic Gold Medals

1996 Atlanta Olympics

Staley's international career reached new heights at the 1996 Atlanta Olympics, where she played a key role in leading Team USA to a gold medal. Her leadership, playmaking ability, and defensive prowess were instrumental in the team's success. Winning an Olympic gold medal was a crowning achievement in Staley's career and showcased her ability to perform on the biggest stage.

2000 Sydney Olympics

Staley continued her international success

at the 2000 Sydney Olympics, where she again helped Team USA secure a gold medal. Her consistency and excellence were evident as she played a vital role in the team's dominance. Staley's performance in Sydney further solidified her reputation as one of the best players in the world.

2004 Athens Olympics

Staley capped off her international playing career with a third gold medal at the 2004 Athens Olympics. Her leadership and experience were invaluable to the team, and she continued to excel in her role. Winning three consecutive Olympic gold medals was a remarkable achievement that underscored Staley's impact on the global stage.

International Competitions and Accolades

FIBA World Championships

In addition to her Olympic success, Staley represented Team USA in multiple FIBA World Championships. Her contributions to these tournaments helped Team USA secure gold medals and maintain its status as the top women's basketball team in the world. Staley's performances in international competitions earned her recognition as one of the greatest players in the history of the sport.

Induction into the Women's Basketball Hall of Fame

Staley's contributions to international basketball were recognized with her induction into the Women's Basketball Hall of Fame. This honor celebrated her impact on the game globally and her role in elevating women's basketball to new heights. Staley's legacy in international basketball is a testament to her exceptional talent and dedication.

Coaching Career Achievements

Dawn Staley's transition from player to coach was seamless, and she quickly established herself as one of the most successful and respected coaches in women's basketball. Her achievements as a coach are a testament to her knowledge of the game, leadership skills, and ability to inspire and develop her players.

Temple University

Turnaround of the Temple Owls
Staley began her coaching career at Temple

University in 2000, while she was still playing in the WNBA. Her impact on the program was immediate, as she led the Temple Owls to unprecedented success. Under her leadership, the team made multiple NCAA tournament appearances and won several Atlantic 10 Conference titles. Staley's ability to transform the program into a contender demonstrated her coaching prowess and set the stage for her future success.

Atlantic 10 Coach of the Year

Staley's success at Temple earned her multiple Atlantic 10 Coach of the Year honors. Her ability to recruit top talent, develop players, and implement effective game strategies made her one of the most respected coaches in the conference. Staley's achievements at Temple laid the foundation for her coaching legacy.

University of South Carolina

Building a National Powerhouse

In 2008, Staley took over as head coach of the University of South Carolina women's basketball team. Her impact on the program was transformative, as she led the Gamecocks to unprecedented success and established them as a national powerhouse.

NCAA Championships

Under Staley's leadership, the Gamecocks won their first NCAA championship in 2017, followed by another championship in 2022. Her ability to build a championship program and guide her team to the pinnacle of college basketball solidified her status as one of the best coaches in the game. Staley's success at South Carolina elevated the program to new heights and brought national recognition to the school.

SEC Championships

In addition to their NCAA championships, the Gamecocks won multiple Southeastern Conference (SEC) titles under Staley's guidance. Her ability to consistently lead her team to success in one of the toughest conferences in college basketball demonstrated her coaching excellence and strategic acumen. Staley's dominance in the SEC was a testament to her recruiting prowess, player development skills, and game preparation.

SEC Coach of the Year

Staley's impact on the SEC did not go unnoticed. She was named SEC Coach of the Year multiple times, reflecting her peers' and the media's recognition of her coaching excellence. Her ability to consistently lead South Carolina to the top of the conference standings and her success in developing elite talent set her apart as one of the premier coaches in the sport.

Player Development and WNBA Draft Success

Staley's success as a coach is also evident in her ability to develop players who succeed at the professional level. Under her guidance, several South Carolina players were drafted into the WNBA, many of whom have gone on to have successful professional careers.

A'ja Wilson

One of the most notable players Staley coached at South Carolina is A'ja Wilson. Under Staley's mentorship, Wilson became one of the most dominant players in college basketball, earning numerous accolades, including the Naismith College Player of the Year award. Wilson's success continued in the WNBA, where she was the first overall pick in the 2018 draft and has since become an MVP and a cornerstone of the Las Vegas Aces.

Alaina Coates and Tyasha Harris

Other notable players Staley developed include Alaina Coates and Tyasha Harris, both of whom were drafted in the first round of the WNBA Draft. Staley's ability to prepare her players for the next level is a significant aspect of her coaching legacy, demonstrating her skill in developing talent that excels on the professional stage.

USA National Team Coaching

Dawn Staley's impact on basketball extends beyond the collegiate level to the international stage, where she has achieved tremendous success as the head coach of the USA Women's National Team.

Olympic Gold Medals

2020 Tokyo Olympics

Staley led the USA Women's National Team to a gold medal at the 2020 Tokyo Olympics. Her ability to manage a team of elite players and navigate the challenges of international competition demonstrated her exceptional coaching skills. Winning the gold medal in Tokyo added another significant achievement to Staley's storied career.

FIBA World Cup

In addition to her Olympic success, Staley has also guided Team USA to victory in the FIBA Women's Basketball World Cup. Her leadership and strategic acumen have helped maintain the USA's dominance in international women's basketball, reinforcing her status as one of the top coaches in the world.

USA Basketball Coach of the Year

Staley's success with the national team has earned her recognition as the USA Basketball Coach of the Year. This honor reflects her contributions to the national program and her ability to lead Team USA to success on the global stage. Staley's impact on international basketball is a testament to her coaching excellence and leadership.

Individual Honors and Awards

Dawn Staley's contributions to basketball have been recognized with numerous individual honors and awards, reflecting her impact on the sport as both a player and a coach.

Naismith Memorial Basketball Hall of Fame

Induction as a Player

In 2013, Staley was inducted into the Naismith Memorial Basketball Hall of Fame as a player. This prestigious honor recognized her exceptional playing career, her impact on the game, and her contributions to the growth of women's basketball. The Hall of Fame induction celebrated Staley's legacy as one of the greatest players in the history of the sport.

Induction as a Coach

In 2021, Staley achieved the rare distinction of being inducted into the Naismith Memorial Basketball Hall of Fame a second time, this time as a coach. This dual recognition highlights her extraordinary success and influence in both playing and coaching roles. Staley's dual induction is a testament to her unparalleled contributions to basketball.

Women's Basketball Hall of Fame

Staley was also inducted into the Women's Basketball Hall of Fame, recognizing her impact on the women's game. This honor celebrated her achievements as a player, coach, and advocate for women's basketball, highlighting her role in advancing the sport and inspiring future generations of female athletes.

State and Local Honors

Philadelphia Sports Hall of Fame

Staley's impact on basketball and her contributions to her hometown of

Philadelphia were recognized with her induction into the Philadelphia Sports Hall of Fame. This honor celebrated her achievements as a player and coach, as well as her influence on the local sports community. Staley's legacy in Philadelphia is a source of pride for the city and its residents.

South Carolina Sports Hall of Fame

In recognition of her success at the University of South Carolina, Staley was inducted into the South Carolina Sports Hall of Fame. This honor reflected her contributions to the state's sports culture and her role in elevating South Carolina's women's basketball program to national prominence.

Advocacy and Contributions to Women's Basketball

Beyond her on-court achievements, Dawn

Staley has made significant contributions to the growth and development of women's basketball through her advocacy and leadership.

Advocacy for Gender Equality

Push for Equal Resources and Opportunities

Staley has been a vocal advocate for gender equality in sports, pushing for equal resources, opportunities, and recognition for female athletes. Her efforts to address disparities in funding, facilities, and media coverage have helped raise awareness and drive change in the sports world. Staley's advocacy work is a vital aspect of her legacy, contributing to a more equitable environment for future generations of female athletes.

Role in Social Justice Initiatives

In addition to her work in gender equality, Staley has been involved in broader social justice initiatives. She has used her platform to advocate for racial equality, inclusion, and social change, addressing issues that impact her players and the wider community. Staley's commitment to social justice reflects her dedication to making a positive impact both on and off the court.

Contributions to the Growth of Women's Basketball

Mentorship and Development Programs

Staley's contributions to women's basketball extend to her mentorship and development programs for young athletes. She has created opportunities for aspiring female basketball players to receive high-quality training, mentorship, and support, helping them achieve their goals and succeed in the sport. Staley's programs have had a profound impact on the development of young talent and the growth of women's basketball.

Influence on Coaching and Leadership

As one of the most successful coaches in women's basketball, Staley has influenced coaching practices and leadership in the sport. Her approach to coaching, which emphasizes player development, empowerment, and excellence, has set a standard for others to follow. Staley's influence on coaching extends beyond her teams, impacting the broader basketball community and inspiring future coaches.

Legacy of Excellence and Inspiration

Dawn Staley's legacy is defined by her

exceptional achievements, her contributions to the growth of women's basketball, and her role as a leader and advocate for positive change. Her impact on the sport is profound and enduring, inspiring countless individuals and shaping the future of women's basketball.

Inspiring Future Generations

Role Model for Aspiring Athletes

Staley's journey from a young girl in Philadelphia to a basketball legend serves as an inspiring example for aspiring athletes. Her dedication, perseverance, and success demonstrate what can be achieved through hard work and determination. Staley's story continues to inspire young athletes to pursue their dreams and strive for excellence.

Mentorship and Leadership

Through her mentorship programs and leadership roles, Staley has directly influenced the lives and careers of many young athletes and coaches. Her guidance and support have helped countless individuals achieve their goals and make a positive impact in their communities. Staley's legacy of mentorship is a lasting testament to her commitment to developing future leaders in the sport.

Lasting Impact on Women's Basketball

Elevating the Sport

Staley's achievements have played a significant role in elevating women's basketball to new heights. Her success as a player and coach has brought greater visibility to the sport, attracting new fans and increasing interest in women's basketball. Staley's contributions have helped pave the way for future generations of female athletes and coaches, ensuring a bright future for the sport.

Commitment to Excellence

Staley's commitment to excellence in all aspects of her career has set a high standard for others to follow. Her dedication to improving her craft, developing her players, and advocating for positive change has left a lasting impact on the basketball community. Staley's legacy is a testament to the power of hard work, passion, and a commitment to making a difference.

Recognition and Honors

Honoring a Basketball Legend

Dawn Staley's numerous awards and honors reflect her extraordinary contributions to the sport of basketball. From her induction into multiple Halls of Fame to her individual accolades as a player and coach, Staley's recognition celebrates her impact on the game and her role as a trailblazer in women's basketball.

Celebrating a Trailblazer

Staley's achievements and contributions have earned her recognition as a trailblazer in women's basketball. Her ability to break barriers, set new standards, and inspire others has made her a revered figure in the sports world. Staley's legacy will continue to be celebrated for generations to come, as her impact on basketball and her influence on the lives of countless individuals endure.

Conclusion

Dawn Staley's career is a remarkable story of achievement, dedication, and impact. Her journey from a young girl in Philadelphia to a basketball legend is marked by numerous career highlights, honors, and records that reflect her exceptional talent and contributions to the sport. As a player, coach, and advocate, Staley has left an indelible mark on women's basketball and inspired countless individuals to pursue their dreams and strive for excellence.

Staley's legacy is defined by her commitment to gender equality, her role in developing future generations of athletes and coaches, and her impact on the growth and visibility of women's basketball. Her achievements and awards celebrate her extraordinary contributions to the game and her lasting influence on the sports world. Dawn Staley's story is a testament to the power of perseverance, passion, and a commitment to making a difference, and her legacy will continue to inspire and shape the future of young generation

CONCLUSION

Dawn Staley's journey through the world of basketball is nothing short of extraordinary. Her story, beginning in the urban landscape of Philadelphia, is a powerful narrative of resilience, talent, and relentless dedication. From the streets where she first dribbled a basketball to the grand arenas where she became a celebrated player and coach, Staley's impact on the sport is profound and multifaceted.

Early Life and Inspiration

Dawn Staley's early life in North Philadelphia laid the foundation for her remarkable career. Growing up in a neighborhood where opportunities were often limited, she found refuge and purpose in basketball. It was here that Staley's innate talent for the game began to shine. Her family's support, especially from her mother, Estelle, was pivotal.

Estelle's encouragement and sacrifices played a crucial role in nurturing Dawn's burgeoning basketball skills. The community courts of Philadelphia served as Staley's first proving grounds, where she honed her competitive spirit and developed the tenacity that would become her hallmark.

High School and Collegiate Stardom

Staley's high school career at Dobbins Technical High School was the first major chapter of her storied journey. Leading her team to multiple Philadelphia Public League titles, she quickly became a local legend. Her exceptional play caught the attention of college scouts across the nation, ultimately

leading her to the University of Virginia (UVA).

At UVA, Staley's legacy continued to grow. She led the Cavaliers to three consecutive NCAA Final Four appearances, a testament to her skill and leadership on the court. Her individual accolades, including two Naismith College Player of the Year awards, solidified her status as one of the greatest players in college basketball history. Staley's time at UVA was marked by not only her athletic prowess but also her academic achievements, reflecting her well-rounded approach to her collegiate experience.

Professional Playing Career

Dawn Staley's transition to professional

basketball saw her excel in both the American Basketball League (ABL) and the Women's National Basketball Association (WNBA). In the ABL, she played for the Richmond Rage and the Philadelphia Rage, earning multiple All-Star selections and showcasing her elite playmaking abilities.

The WNBA provided a larger stage for Staley's talents. As a member of the Charlotte Sting and later the Houston Comets, she continued to amass accolades, including multiple WNBA All-Star appearances. Staley's leadership and court vision were instrumental in her teams' successes, and she became known for her ability to elevate the play of those around her. Her professional career was a continuation of the excellence she had demonstrated at every level of the sport.

International Success with Team USA

Staley's impact on basketball extended beyond the United States. As a member of Team USA, she represented her country with distinction in international competitions. Her career with Team USA is highlighted by three Olympic gold medals, won in 1996 (Atlanta), 2000 (Sydney), and 2004 (Athens). These achievements underscored her status as one of the world's elite players and cemented her legacy on the global stage.

Staley's international career also included success in the FIBA Women's Basketball World Cup, where she helped Team USA secure multiple gold medals. Her contributions to these victories were characterized by her leadership, poise under pressure, and unmatched court intelligence. Representing her country was a source of immense pride for Staley, and she approached each competition with the same intensity and determination that defined her entire career.

Transition to Coaching

While still an active player, Dawn Staley embarked on a coaching career that would eventually eclipse even her playing achievements. She began her coaching journey at Temple University, where she quickly transformed the program. Under her leadership, Temple's women's basketball team made several NCAA tournament appearances, signaling the arrival of a new coaching star.

In 2008, Staley accepted the head coaching position at the University of South Carolina, a move that would elevate her to legendary status in the coaching ranks. Her tenure at South Carolina has been marked by unprecedented success. Staley's ability to recruit top talent, develop players, and foster a winning culture led the Gamecocks to their first NCAA championship in 2017.

Her coaching philosophy, emphasizing discipline, teamwork, and resilience, resonated with her players and transformed the program into a perennial powerhouse.

Coaching Team USA

Staley's coaching prowess extended to the international arena when she was named head coach of the USA Women's National Team. Under her leadership, Team USA continued its dominance in international competitions, capturing gold at the 2020 Tokyo Olympics. Staley's success as a coach on the global stage mirrored her achievements as a player, demonstrating her deep understanding of the game and her ability to lead at the highest levels.

Her tenure as Team USA coach also included victories in the FIBA Women's Basketball World Cup, further cementing her legacy as one of the sport's premier coaches. Staley's impact on the international stage is a testament to her strategic acumen, ability to inspire her players, and unwavering commitment to excellence.

Advocacy and Philanthropy

Beyond her on-court achievements, Dawn Staley has made significant contributions off the court. She is a passionate advocate for gender equality, using her platform to push for equal resources, opportunities, and recognition for female athletes. Staley's advocacy extends to social justice issues, where she has been a vocal proponent of racial equality and inclusion. Her efforts have helped raise awareness and drive change within the sports community and beyond.

Staley's philanthropic endeavors are also noteworthy. Through the Dawn Staley Foundation, she has created programs that support underprivileged youth, providing them with opportunities to succeed both in sports and in life. Her commitment to giving back to the community reflects her belief in the power of sports to effect positive change and her desire to make a lasting impact beyond her own career.

Honors and Recognition

Dawn Staley's contributions to basketball have been recognized with numerous honors and awards. Her induction into the Naismith Memorial Basketball Hall of Fame as both a player (2013) and coach (2021) is a rare and prestigious achievement, highlighting her exceptional impact on the sport in multiple capacities. She has also been inducted into the Women's Basketball Hall of Fame and the Philadelphia Sports Hall of Fame, among others.

Staley's awards and accolades celebrate not only her individual accomplishments but also her influence on the game as a whole. These honors are a testament to her skill, leadership, and dedication to advancing women's basketball. Staley's legacy is further reflected in the success of her former players, many of whom have gone on to have impactful careers in the WNBA and beyond.

Lasting Impact and Legacy

Dawn Staley's legacy is defined by her ability to inspire and mentor the next generation of athletes and coaches. Her journey from a young girl in Philadelphia to a basketball legend serves as a powerful example of what can be achieved through hard work, determination, and a commitment to excellence. Staley's story continues to inspire young athletes to pursue their dreams and strive for greatness.

As a coach, Staley has influenced the lives and careers of many players, helping them develop their skills and reach their full potential. Her approach to coaching, which emphasizes player development, empowerment, and excellence, has set a standard for others to follow. Staley's influence on coaching extends beyond her teams, impacting the broader basketball community and inspiring future coaches to adopt her principles.

Staley's contributions to the growth of women's basketball are profound. Her success has brought greater visibility to the sport, attracting new fans and increasing interest in women's basketball. Her advocacy for gender equality and social justice has helped create a more equitable environment for future generations of female athletes. Staley's legacy is a testament to the power of sports to effect positive change and the enduring impact of her contributions to the game.

Conclusion

Dawn Staley's career is a remarkable story of triumphs, contributions, and enduring impact. From her early days in Philadelphia to her illustrious playing and coaching career, Staley has consistently demonstrated excellence on and off the basketball court. Her journey is marked by numerous achievements, including NCAA Final Four appearances, WNBA All-Star selections, Olympic gold medals, and coaching successes at the collegiate and international levels.

Staley's influence extends beyond her on-court accomplishments. As an advocate for gender equality and social justice, she has used her platform to drive positive change within the sports community and beyond. Her philanthropic efforts and commitment to giving back reflect her belief in the power of sports to make a difference in people's lives.

The numerous honors and awards she has received underscore her significant impact on the sport of basketball. Staley's legacy is defined by her ability to inspire and mentor future generations of athletes and coaches, her contributions to the growth and visibility of women's basketball, and her commitment to excellence in all aspects of her career. Her story is a powerful example of what can be achieved through hard work, determination, and a relentless pursuit of greatness.

Dawn Staley's legacy will continue to inspire countless individuals, and her influence will be felt for many years to come. As a player, coach, and advocate, Dawn Staley embodies the spirit of excellence and leadership, making her a true icon in the world of sports. Her impact on basketball and her contributions to society are enduring testaments to her remarkable career and the lasting difference she has made.

APPENDIX

Timeline of Dawn Staley's Career

Early Years and High School (1970s-1988)

- 1970: Dawn Michelle Staley is born on May 4, 1970, in Philadelphia, Pennsylvania.

- 1984-1988: Attends Dobbins Technical High School in Philadelphia, where she excels in basketball.

- 1988: Leads Dobbins Tech to multiple Philadelphia Public League championships.

Collegiate Career at the University of Virginia (1988-1992)

1988-1989: Freshman Year

- Earns a basketball scholarship to the University of Virginia (UVA).
- Makes an immediate impact, averaging double figures in points and assists.

1989-1990: Sophomore Year

- Leads UVA to the NCAA Final Four, earning All-American honors.
- Named ACC Player of the Year.

1990-1991: Junior Year
- UVA returns to the NCAA Final Four, Staley

wins her first Naismith College Player of the Year award.

1991-1992: Senior Year

- UVA reaches the NCAA Final Four for the third consecutive year.
- Staley wins her second Naismith College Player of the Year award.
- Graduates from UVA with numerous school records, including career assists.

Professional Playing Career (1996-2006)

1996-1999: American Basketball League (ABL)

- Drafted by the Richmond Rage in the inaugural season of the ABL.

- Named to the ABL All-Star team multiple times.
- Plays for the Philadelphia Rage after the Richmond franchise folds.

1997-2006: Women's National Basketball Association (WNBA)

- Drafted by the Charlotte Sting as the ninth overall pick in the 1999 WNBA Draft.
- Plays for the Charlotte Sting (1999-2005) and Houston Comets (2005-2006).
- Named to multiple WNBA All-Star teams.
- Retires as one of the most respected point guards in WNBA history.

International Career with Team USA (1989-2004)

1989: Begins representing Team USA in international competitions.
- Wins gold at the 1989 FIBA World Championship.

1996: Atlanta Olympics

- Wins her first Olympic gold medal with Team USA.

2000: Sydney Olympics

- Wins her second Olympic gold medal.

2004: Athens Olympics

- Wins her third Olympic gold medal.

Coaching Career (2000-present)

2000-2008: Temple University

- Begins coaching career at Temple while still playing in the WNBA.
- Leads Temple to several NCAA tournament appearances.

2008-present: University of South Carolina

- Hired as head coach of the University of South Carolina women's basketball team.
- Leads the Gamecocks to their first NCAA championship in 2017.
- Builds South Carolina into a perennial powerhouse in women's college basketball.
- Named SEC Coach of the Year multiple times.

Coaching Team USA (2017-present)

2017: Named head coach of the USA Women's National Team.
- Leads Team USA to a gold medal at the 2020 Tokyo Olympics.
- Guides Team USA to success in various FIBA World Cup tournaments.

Off the Court Activities and Honors

- **Philanthropy:** Establishes the Dawn Staley Foundation to support underprivileged youth.
- **Advocacy:** Promotes gender equality and social justice initiatives in sports.
- **Hall of Fame Inductions:** Inducted into the Naismith Memorial Basketball Hall of Fame as both a player (2013) and coach (2021).
- **National Recognition:** Receives numerous awards for her contributions to basketball and society.

Legacy and Impact

- Inspires a generation of athletes through her dedication, leadership, and resilience.
- Continues to influence the growth of women's basketball globally.
- Recognized as a pioneer in the sport, breaking barriers on and off the court.

Made in the USA
Middletown, DE
04 April 2025

73779977R00146